WOMEN in POLITICS

Benazir Bhutto

Women in Politics

WOMEN in POLITICS

Benazir Bhutto

Mercedes Padrino

CHELSEA HOUSE
PUBLISHERS
A Haights Cross Communications Company
Philadelphia

CHELSEA HOUSE PUBLISHERS
VP, New Product Development Sally Cheney
Director of Production Kim Shinners
Creative Manager Takeshi Takahashi
Manufacturing Manager Diann Grasse

Staff for BENAZIR BHUTTO
Executive Editor Lee Marcott
Associate Editor Kate Sullivan
Production Editor Megan Emery
Photo Editor Sarah Bloom
Series & Cover Designer Terry Mallon
Layout 21st Century Publishing and Communications, Inc.

www.chelseahouse.com

First Printing

9 8 7 6 5 4 3 2 1

Library of Congress Cataloging-in-Publication Data

Anderson, Mercedes Padrino.
   Benazir Bhutto / by Mercedes Padrino [Anderson].
      v. cm. — (Women in politics)
   Includes bibliographical references and index.
   Contents: The election, 1988 — A sheltered and privileged childhood,
1953-1969 — Time in the West, 1969-1977 — Thrust into politics,
1977-1979 — Imprisonment and exile, 1979-1987 — Mohtarma, 1987-
1993 — A second chance, 1993-1997 — The work continues, 1997-pre-
sent — Chronology.
   ISBN 0-7910-7732-2 (hardcover) — ISBN 0-7910-8000-5 (pbk.) 1.
Bhutto, Benazir—Juvenile literature. 2. Prime ministers—Pakistan—
Biography—Juvenile literature. [1. Bhutto, Benazir. 2. Prime ministers.
3. Pakistan—Politics and government. 4. Women—Biography.] I. Title.
II. Series.
   DS389.22.B48A54 2004
   954.9105'092—dc22

                                                    2003028102

Table of Contents

Benazir Bhutto

1

The Election

1988

I always knew Benazir would do well. And I thought her eventual leadership of Pakistan—assuming she was permitted to live—became inevitable on April 4, 1979, when under the military dictatorship of General Mohammed Zia ul-Haq, her father was hanged.

—Peter W. Galbraith[1]

For 16 anxious days, Benazir Bhutto and the Pakistan People's Party (PPP) waited for President Ghulam Ishaq Khan to ask them to form a government. They had won 94 of the 207 seats in the National Assembly (NA)—more than any other party. When Bhutto first heard the results, she experienced "a moment of sheer happiness,"[2] but although she had already told the press that the PPP had won the election and that, as its leader, she expected to become prime minister, she could not be sure that things would turn out as she wished. The

The Pakistan People's Party (PPP), founded by Bhutto's father, earned more votes in the 1988 election than any other party. As leader of the PPP, Bhutto expected to become Pakistan's prime minister—but President Ishaq Khan blocked her. She responded by forming a coalition between the PPP and another party that gave the PPP a clear majority in the National Assembly. Nevertheless, two long weeks passed before President Ishaq Khan recognized the victory and Bhutto became the youngest chief executive in the world.

army and the caretaker government that was running the country until the elected representatives were sworn in did not want her in power.

In a parliamentary system like Pakistan's, the party that wins the majority of seats is normally asked to form a government. If no party gets a majority—more than half—of the seats, then the party that gets a plurality (the highest number of votes that does not exceed half), like the PPP in November 1988, is asked to form a coalition government with other parties. Instead of following normal practice, however, President Ghulam Ishaq Khan looked for a way to put the government in the hands of his political allies.

Bhutto, however, was not the type of person to sit doing nothing. She rapidly negotiated a coalition with another party, the Mohajir Quami Movement (MQM), and several independent members that gave her 108 votes in the National Assembly— a bare majority but a real one. Then she paced the floor and waited. Still, Ishaq Khan dawdled. The public did not like the delay, and even newspapers that had supported other parties called on the president to hand the government over to the PPP. Finally, 13 days after the election, the American ambassador informed Ishaq Khan that the United States—Pakistan's most important ally—expected him to allow Bhutto to become prime minister. The president was forced to give in.

On the afternoon of December 1, 1988, Bhutto walked into the audience hall of the presidential palace to be sworn in. She wore the colors of the Pakistani flag: emerald green and white. As prayers were said and Bhutto took the oath of office, her mother wept. Bhutto later recalled,

[T]he most exciting moment in my life was when I was sworn in as Prime Minister. I remember walking down the red carpet in the presidential palace and I felt as though an invisible army of all those who had died fighting for freedom walked with me and it was a tremendous moment of vindication. I also felt a tremendous sense that Pakistan had showed the way for other Muslim countries, that a woman could be elected as chief executive.[3]

The audience before her, however, was made up of political enemies as well as the friends and well-wishers. As she looked around, she wondered if she could trust the people she would have to work with—people who had been the allies of the dictator who executed her father, the last popularly elected prime minister. Nonetheless, she gave a hopeful speech, promising, "My government . . . [will] strive for building a progressive and democratic Pakistan, free from all kinds of exploitation," a government that would "promote the lofty Islamic principles of amity, brotherhood, equality and tolerance."[4] She reminded her many poor constituents, "We are from amongst you. Your suffering, happiness and honor is our suffering, happiness and honor."[5]

Bhutto knew that she was facing a very difficult challenge, that some in the PPP believed that it would have been better to go into the National Assembly as the strong opposition party that could act as the government's conscience. After ten years

ARMY INTERVENTIONS

Pakistan was founded in 1947, and the Pakistani army has been involved in civilian affairs since 1953. That year, when the police could not control religious violence that was spreading through the Punjab, the civilian authorities asked the army to intervene. Over the years, the army took an increasingly active role in government. The military has taken over the government of Pakistan on four different occasions. Each time, the generals claimed that the civilian government was ineffective or corrupt. Even when civilians are permitted to govern Pakistan, the army still decides national policy about certain issues. When Benazir Bhutto, then prime minister, was asked if she would cut the military budget, she answered, "Not unless we want the army to take over again."*

* Owen Bennett Jones, *Pakistan: Eye of the Storm.* New Haven, Conn.: Yale University Press, 2002, p. 237.

of prison, exile, and battling a dictator, however, Bhutto was eager to forge a new Pakistan according to democratic principles. She accepted the challenge—even though she had no experience in government. It was not in her character to back away. One ambassador with a critical eye described her thus:

> She's one of the most bewildering women I've ever met: one moment, she is utter charm; the next moment, she's so antagonistic that she comes perilously close to impertinence. But she's not a sulker; she's a battler and a survivor, and that's not all bad. Basically, she's driven. . . . She'll do anything to get elected, and she simply cannot accept that anyone can do this country any good except her.[6]

A former minister, Iqbal Akhund, took a kinder view: "She was by no means boastful in private—rather the contrary. Sometimes the arrogance and peremptory manner only reflected impatience with and mistrust (often perfectly justified) of the establishment and its ways."[7]

During a visit before she became prime minister, Akhund saw another quality that lay behind Bhutto's self-confidence and drive: "[T]here was about her also an aura of loneliness— an elemental kind of inner loneliness."[8]

2

A Sheltered and Privileged Childhood

1953–1969

I found that [my father] . . . would always be so pleased when I did well. . . . I'd have a neat handwriting. . . . I'd get my work done and finish everything. I was very studious.

—Benazir Bhutto [9]

Sindh province is in southeastern Pakistan, west of India, and washed by the waters of the Arabian Sea. It is the location of the ancient city of Mohenjo-Daro, which dates from about 2500 B.C., contemporaneous with ancient Egypt. In Larkana, near Mohenjo-Daro, the Bhutto family had its country home and lands that stretched for miles. The family home was called Al-Murtaza. Benazir Bhutto recalled, "My brothers, sister, and I took great pride that we had been raised in the shadow of [Mohenjo-Daro], that we lived on the bank of the Indus, which had been bringing life to the land since the beginning of time." [10]

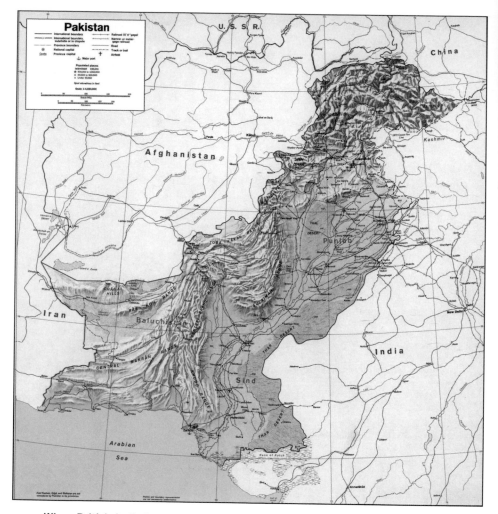

When British India became independent in 1947, Great Britain divided the territory into a secular India, which in fact was mainly Hindu, and the two Muslim territories of East Pakistan and West Pakistan. East Pakistan, located across India on the Bay of Bengal, separated to become Bangladesh in 1971. Modern Pakistan is divided into two territories and its four provinces—Balochistan in the southwest, Punjab in the east, Sindh in the southeast, and the Northwest Frontier Province. Jammu and Kashmir, northeast of Islamabad, is a site of perpetual conflict with India. Benazir Bhutto is from Karachi, on the southern coast.

Bhutto's grandfather, Sir Shah Nawaz Bhutto, began the custom of moving the family to Karachi for most of the year. Her grandmother built a house at 70 Clifton, near the beach, soon after Benazir was born on June 21, 1953. Karachi was the national capital at that time, and its busy port serviced both Pakistan and Afghanistan. Bhutto remembered the city of her childhood:

> It was a very different world then. Very few motor cars and much more poverty. The gap between the rich and the poor was greater too. I remember people walking barefoot and bare-backed because of the poverty. . . . I remember that the poorer people would greet the richer people by bending down and touching their feet, or prostrating . . . and throwing themselves on the feet, so it was a totally different kind of world and it has changed for the better.'" [11]

The Bhuttos were members of the feudal class, with numerous servants who attended to their needs and comforts. With an ancestry dating back to the earliest Muslim warriors in the subcontinent, they were accustomed to exercising authority. Like feudal lords in other parts of the world, the Bhuttos and other landowners were protective of their property, honor, and privileges. Because Muslim women—not only men—inherit property, Bhutto cousins had married each other for generations to keep control of their lands. When no male cousins were available for marriage, daughters were forced to remain single, living in purdah, or seclusion from strangers. Benazir had four aunts who lived this way in their own compound, going out only for special occasions and receiving family visitors at home.

The feudals did not value formal education highly. Besides religious instruction, boys merely needed to know how to run their future estates and girls how to manage a household, but no other schooling was considered necessary or even desirable.

Sir Shah Nawaz Bhutto, however, was a modern, far-seeing man who sent his children to school and arranged marriages for his younger daughters outside the family. He sent his son, Zulfikar, to the United States for college, where he graduated from the University of California at Berkeley, and to Oxford University in England, where he received his law degree. Sir Shah Nawaz Bhutto also wanted to set an example for other landowners. He was the first Bhutto to become politically active and had a distinguished career under British rule.

On her mother's side, Benazir's family was very different. Her paternal grandfather, Mirza Muhammad Isphahani, was an Iranian who had established a soap business in Bombay. Benazir's mother, Nusrat, and her sisters received a sophisticated, urban upbringing. They were formally educated, drove automobiles, and were not required to wear veils to go outside. In 1947, after the partition of India, the family resettled in Karachi, where Nusrat joined the Pakistan Women's National Guard, rising to the rank of captain.

FEUDALISM

The feudal landowners of Pakistan are similar to the feudal lords of medieval Europe. Most—although not all—own huge tracts of land that is worked by illiterate peasants who are often bonded laborers or serfs. The feudals have traditionally commanded great loyalty and exercised authority over the people on their lands. The serfs defend their lords against enemies and take orders only from the lords or their surrogates. In many places, the feudals are considered religious leaders and also act as justices of the peace, granting divorces, settling disputes, and putting criminals in private jails or meting out other punishments, especially in remote areas. The feudals, who are a small minority of the population, are one of the few literate groups in the country. They maintain close ties to civil servants and the military and thus access to power. Most legislators come from the feudal class.

When she married Zulfikar Ali Bhutto, Nusrat Isphahani's life changed dramatically. She went into purdah in the Bhutto household, going out only to visit her own family and always under a head-to-toe veil called a burka. Things soon changed, however. Benazir's grandmother liked having a daughter-in-law who could drive her places without waiting for a male chauffer to become available, and, when she had 70 Clifton built, it was designed so the entire family lived together, without separate quarters for men and women.

HOME AND SCHOOLS

Benazir, nicknamed Pinkie, was the oldest of four children. Her brother Mir Murtaza, born in 1954, was a year younger. Her sister Sanam, called Sunny, arrived in 1957, and the youngest, her brother Shah Nawaz, in 1958. When Benazir was young, three generations lived at 70 Clifton, where she was surrounded by affection. She would spend the afternoons with her grandparents in the garden and has said, "I don't remember my grandparents ever scold[ing] me."[12] Her mother's family lived within walking distance, and Benazir visited with them often. Her maternal grandfather would take her to stores to buy her treats and let her pick the fruit off the trees in his garden.

At age three, Benazir went to nursery school, and in 1958, she was enrolled at the Convent of Jesus and Mary, a private school. The nuns taught classes in English, the language spoken most often at the Bhutto home. Benazir was actually growing up in a multilingual atmosphere: Her home language was Sindhi, and her mother's family spoke Persian, the language of Iran.

In many ways, Benazir had a typical childhood. She got into trouble at times for breaking something or doing what she had been told not to do, and she liked to dress up in her parents' clothes. In other ways, however, her upbringing was unusual. By the time she was four, her father was already deeply involved in government affairs. During her middle childhood, Benazir said, "I saw my father as much on the front pages of the newspapers as in person." [13] The children were left in the care of their governess.

From a very early age, Benazir's parents instilled in her a sense of responsibility. As the oldest child, she was told to mind her brothers and sister. Benazir and her sister, Sanam, also had an unusual upbringing in another way: They were served their meals with their brothers rather than waiting for the boys to finish eating and then getting the leftovers, as in many households. Benazir explained, "There was no question in my family that my sister and I would be given the same opportunities in life as our brothers. Nor was there in Islam. We learned at an early age that it was men's interpretation of our religion that restricted women's opportunities, not our religion itself." [14] For the Bhuttos, the most important of these opportunities was education. Zulfikar Bhutto used to tell his children, "I ask only one thing of you, that you do well in your studies." [15] All of them were expected to put in extra effort to improve themselves. Their parents brought in tutors who worked with them on English, math, and religion in the afternoons after school. Moreover, their father intended for his children—including his girls—to follow in his footsteps and attend universities abroad.

When the national capital moved from Karachi to Rawalpindi in 1959, the Bhutto family moved there. At first life was rather lonely for Benazir. She did not know any of the girls at her new school, her grandparents had died, and there were no other relatives to fill the house. Soon the family began going on picnics on Sundays near the ancient city of Taxila, and when her aunt's family moved to Rawalpindi, they would get together for boating parties. Her father took Benazir to the bookstore in Rawalpindi and bought her books. She also began to develop her own interests. She became a stamp collector and an avid reader of biographies and Agatha Christie mysteries. Benazir particularly enjoyed reading about historical figures who had overcome difficulties in order to accomplish something. Sanam Bhutto remembered how

Benazir "was fond of making cakes, especially when the parents were not around."[16]

When Benazir was ten, the children's governess resigned to return to England. The Bhuttos then placed the children in boarding schools, in part because Zulfikar Bhutto thought it would be a good experience for them to live without the comforts of home. The girls were sent to a school in the Murree hills, where, as Benazir says, "For the first time I had to make my own bed, polish my shoes, carry water for bathing and toothbrushing back and forth from the water taps in the corridors."[17] On their weekly visits with their parents, the girls complained about the poor bathroom facilities, and eventually new bathrooms were built for the students.

In September 1965, war broke out between Pakistan and India over Kashmir, a large region between the two countries that had once been an independent principality and that both countries wanted to control. The road to Kashmir crossed the Murree hills, and many people feared that the Indian army might overrun the disputed region and march into Pakistan through the area. For the girls at the school, it was a period of both fear and excitement. Benazir related,

> [N]ow suddenly we had air-raid practices and blackouts. The nuns made the older sisters responsible for getting their younger sisters into the shelters, and I made Sunny tie her slippers to her feet at night so she wouldn't lose time looking for them. Many of our schoolmates were daughters of prominent government officials or army officers, and with excitement we gave each other false names and practiced them in case we fell into the hands of our enemies. . . . For the seventeen days of the war, the threat of invasion was quite real and frightening.[18]

The peace settlement stopped the immediate fighting, but it was controversial and did not resolve the disagreement over Kashmir.

By and large, Benazir enjoyed her two years at Murree. She was a good student, played sports, and made friends. Sanam, on the other hand, was very unhappy, so the Bhuttos removed their daughters from Murree and reenrolled them at the Presentation Convent in Rawalpindi.

The nuns who taught Benazir were an important influence in her life. To this day, she remembers Mother Eugene, her literature teacher at the Convent of Jesus and Mary: "Mother Eugene used to teach us literature and poetry, and to reach for the moon, and the lodestar. . . . It was very inspirational and motivational that one could conquer the moon and the stars if one reached out." [19]

ZULFIKAR AND NUSRAT BHUTTO

Nusrat Bhutto guided the children on the daily practice of their faith. Although the Bhuttos were Sunni Muslims, Nusrat was Shiite, like most Iranians. (The differences between the two branches of Islam center around orthodoxy—conforming to the established doctrines of the faith—and who was the rightful successor to Mohammed, the founder of the religion.) The differences did not present a problem for the family, however. Nusrat Bhutto was very devout, and even when she was traveling to other parts of the world, she stopped to face Mecca and say the five daily prayers. As Benazir grew up, her mother showed her how to join in the different rituals. "When I was nine years old, she began to include me, slipping into my bedroom to lead me in the morning prayer." [20] As Benazir grew older, Nusrat included her in communal rituals with other women.

Benazir's relationship with her mother was complex. While the family lived in Rawalpindi, her parents had marital problems that led to a separation, and Nusrat Bhutto went to stay with relatives in Iran. Although her parents reconciled and her mother returned, Benazir remained troubled by the possibility of future family problems: "I was always afraid that she . . . [might] leave us again." [21]Her mother was also the more socially conservative parent, in spite of her sophisticated upbringing. Says Benazir, "it was my mother who taught that a woman grew up to be married and to have children, and she would tell my father in front of me, 'Why do you want to educate her? No man will want to marry her.'" [22]

When Benazir became an adolescent, her mother followed Bhutto family tradition and provided her with a burka. Benazir described the experience:

> I passed from childhood into the world of the adult. But what a disappointing world it turned out to be. The colors of the sky, the grass, the flowers were gone, muted and grayish. Everything was blurred by the pattern over my eyes. . . . The fabric which covered me from head to toe made it difficult to walk. Shut off from whatever breeze there might be, the sweat began to pour down my face.[23]

To her relief, her father did not think she should wear the burka, and she was allowed to break with tradition.

From a very early age, Zulfikar Bhutto tried to develop a political consciousness in his children. He would tell them about important people and world events. When U.S. President John F. Kennedy was shot in November 1963, he woke Benazir up to tell her the news and have her follow the reports with him through the night. He also had the children meet foreign visitors whenever possible, although the children did not always appreciate the significance of the visits or the people they met. Zulfikar taught his children about politics even when they were apart. While the girls were in boarding school in Murree, he discussed politics in his letters to them.

Early in 1966, Zulfikar Bhutto resigned from President Ayub Khan's cabinet over the Kashmir peace agreement Ayub

Khan had accepted with India. The country's widespread poverty and social inequality, combined with the disappointment over Kashmir, led to political unrest in many parts of the country. At the same time, Bhutto's personal popularity soared. In June, the Bhutto family returned to Karachi. Crowds met their train along the way, running alongside and shouting, "Long live Bhutto!"

In 1967, Bhutto founded the Pakistan People's Party (PPP) with the populist motto of *Roti, Kapra, aum Makan* which meant "bread, clothing, and shelter." Bhutto toured Pakistan, speaking to the poor and disenfranchised, to laborers and women, urging them to demand their rights. Benazir's political conscience thus began to develop. "Terms such as 'cold war' and 'arms embargo' had already become part of our dimly understood vocabulary as small children. . . . But after my father broke with Ayub Khan in 1966, the words 'civil liberties' and 'democracy' were the ones that came up most. . . ."[24] On visits to their family land, her father would say to the children, "Look at the way these people sweat in the heat and in the sun in the fields, and it is because of their sweat that you will have the opportunity to be educated." He would add, "You have a debt and you've got to come back and pay that debt by serving your people."[25]

At first, Ayub Khan's government tried to cajole Bhutto into giving up his political activities. In time, the offers to promote his political career if he cooperated turned into threats against his life. For the first time, the realities of political life came home to Benazir. "Our house became filled with tension, but I tried not to show my fear. What good would it have done? This was the life of politics in Pakistan, and therefore the life we led. . . . I didn't even allow myself to feel frightened. I tried, in fact, not to feel anything at all."[26] As 1968 wore on, antigovernment demonstrations and violence increased, and, in November, Zulfikar Bhutto and other PPP leaders were arrested.

Bhutto's father, Zulfikar Ali Bhutto (1928–1979), was born in British India and educated in Bombay, the United States, and Great Britain. He married Nusrat Isphahani in 1951, and Benazir Bhutto was born in Karachi two years later. He became Pakistan's foreign minister in 1963 and left this position in 1967 to found the PPP. After the war with India, he served temporarily as president and then as prime minister.

Meanwhile, Benazir was trying to prepare for her college entrance exams. To graduate and go to college, she also had to pass the O-level exams. From prison, her father wrote to her,

"I am praying for your success in your O-level examinations.
I am really proud to have a daughter who is so bright that she
is doing O-levels at the young age of fifteen, three years before
I did them. At this rate, you might become president."[27]

Instructing Benazir to "stay in Karachi and study," Nusrat
Bhutto went to Lahore with Benazir's siblings to file the necessary
papers at the High Court to have her husband released from
prison. She also led many marches protesting her husband's
imprisonment. Benazir was lonely: "I wanted more than anything to be in Lahore with my family."[28]

Nevertheless, Benazir obeyed her mother:

> I buried myself in my work, going over and over my
> subjects with the tutors who came to the house every day.
> In the evenings I sometimes joined my friends Fifi,
> Thamineh, Fatime, and Samiya at the nearby Sindh Club.
> . . . We played squash and swam in the pool, though we all
> knew things were not as carefree as they seemed. Ever since
> my father had started challenging Ayub, some of my
> friends' relatives and "well-wishers" had begun cautioning
> them that friendship with the Bhuttos was dangerous. . . .
> Samiya's father had been warned . . . that his daughter's
> friendship with me could bring trouble to his family.[29]

After being released from prison in early 1969, Zulfikar
Bhutto staged a hunger strike to continue putting pressure on
Ayub Khan. In March, in the midst of unrest, the president
finally resigned but did not call for elections. Rather, he named
General Yahya Khan as his successor. Yahya Khan ruled under
martial law—rule by the military in which civil rights are
suspended—but called for elections to be held in December
1970. For the Bhuttos and the Pakistan People's Party, the
election campaign began.

Benazir took her exams and applied to college. When an
acceptance letter from Radcliffe College arrived, Benazir was

not sure that it was the best time for her to go to the United States for four years. With so much political uncertainty, she wanted to be near her family. Moreover, the college had advised her parents that at age 16, she might not be mature enough for college. Her father, however, did not want her to waste any time. He gave his daughter a beautiful new Koran as a parting gift, and, in August 1969, her mother took Benazir to the United States to begin her new life.

3

Time in the West
1969–1977

There is a fiction that what has happened could not have been foreseen.
. . . But people who knew Benazir Bhutto well found her fairly amazing
even at eighteen.

—a Harvard classmate[30]

When Benazir arrived in Cambridge, Massachusetts, to begin her college studies, Radcliffe was Harvard University's school for women. Radcliffe undergraduates had classes with the male undergraduates from Harvard College but lived in separate dormitories. Benazir was assigned to Eliot Hall. She had a roommate with whom she shared a bedroom, and all the girls on the floor shared a bathroom off the hallway.

Nusrat Bhutto stayed in the United States for several weeks to make sure Benazir was comfortable so far from home, and she determined the direction of Mecca from Benazir's room so her daughter would be able to say prayers. She also put Benazir in touch with Professor John Kenneth Galbraith and his wife. Galbraith had served as United States ambassador to India and was a friend of Zulfikar Bhutto's.

ADAPTING TO A DIFFERENT CULTURE

Her early days in Cambridge were an adventure for Benazir. Her classmates were friendly, and she delighted in doing American things and taking part in student life. "I drank gallons of apple cider, ate unconscionable numbers of peppermint stick ice-cream cones . . . from Brigham's ice cream parlor, and regularly attended rock concerts in Boston as well as the garden parties at Professor and Mrs. Galbraith's. . . . I loved the novelty of America."[31]

At the same time, however, Benazir was frustrated by her fellow student's complete ignorance about Pakistan. Out of approximately 300 women in her class, only 5 were from foreign countries. None of the American girls seemed to have heard of her country and only developed a vague idea when she told them it was the largest Muslim country in the world and explained its proximity to India. It was a painful explanation to have to give:

> I smarted every time I heard . . . [others show knowledge about] India, with whom we had had two bitter wars. Pakistan was supposed to be one of America's strongest allies, a geographical buffer against the Soviet influence in India and our other border countries of Communist China, Afghanistan, and Iran. The United States used our air bases in northern Pakistan. . . . Yet Americans seemed completely unaware even of the existence of my country.[32]

Benazir was also shocked by the dress and behavior of young Americans. One of her Harvard classmates was Peter

Galbraith, Professor Galbraith's son. "To my sheltered and conservative eye," she explained, "Peter Galbraith seemed shocking. His hair was long, he was dressed in old and untidy clothes, and he smoked cigarettes in front of his parents. He looked more like a waif the former ambassador to India had brought home with him than the son of a senior diplomat and respected professor."[33] Soon enough, however, Benazir adopted some shocking American ways herself. She let her hair grow long, and wore it straight with bangs like the other girls. She packed away the traditional Pakistani tunics and loose trousers that she had taken to college and bought sweatshirts and jeans.

At Harvard, Benazir discovered that being Pinkie from Pakistan, a country no one knew anything about, could have real advantages. At home, her last name gave her instant recognition and raised expectations about how she should behave and how others should behave toward her, which made Benazir always feel shy among strangers. In Cambridge, she forced herself to set aside her shyness and learned to get around Harvard like any ordinary young woman. "At first I had to ask directions to the library, to the lecture halls, the dorms. I couldn't afford to be tongue-tied. I had been thrown into the deep end of a strange and foreign pool. If I were to get to the surface, I had to get there by myself."[34]

During her freshman year, she also learned a painful lesson in self-sufficiency. Over winter break, she was left alone at Radcliffe when her friends went home to celebrate the holidays. She was extremely lonely with neither friends nor family near her for many days, but she found a way to cope that would serve her well during the years of imprisonment and exile that were to come. "Somehow when you are active and doing a lot of things you don't have time to think." So she learned not to "sit and mourn where I am. I just adjust myself to the circumstances and the place where I am."[35] She filled her time with the theater, movies, reading, and writing.

Her first year at Harvard was generally a happy one. She was conscientious about her work, although it was a setback to get a C on one of her first semester finals. "I was so ashamed of myself.... I wondered what my father would think of me...."[36] Benazir adapted to campus life and joined various different extracurricular groups. According to Peter Galbraith, "In many ways she was like the other women in our class: bright, and determined to be a full participant, not an observer, in undergraduate life." He added, "[She] spoke up in class, and more than held her own in dining-hall debates."[37]

Benazir also got involved in politics. She took part in demonstrations against the Vietnam War, even though she feared that, as a foreigner, she might be deported for doing so. "I had opposed the Vietnam War at home and was becoming even more radicalized by the antiwar fever in America."[38] She worked for less contentious causes as well, helping raise money for the victims of the cyclone that hit East Pakistan (the future Bangladesh) that year. She earned her first speaker's fee from a speech she gave on that subject. Benazir also had the pleasure of seeing a letter published that she wrote to the editor of *Life* objecting to an article about the Aswan Dam in Egypt.

One of Benazir's dearest political causes was the women's liberation movement, which was then getting started. For Benazir, the women's movement was both politically and personally liberating:

> Night after night my friends and I gathered to talk about our aspirations for our futures and the definition of the new relationships we would strike with whomever we married—if indeed we chose to get married at all. In Pakistan I had been among the minority who didn't view marriage and family as their primary goal. At Harvard I was amongst a sea of women who felt as unimpeded by their gender as I did.[39]

At the same time, Benazir's father continued to groom her for a career in politics. Her parents sent her newspapers from Pakistan every week. Zulfikar Bhutto wanted her to study political science, but Benazir was at first attracted to psychology. She recalled, "[W]hen I discovered that the major entailed courses in medical sciences and the dissection of animals, I turned squeamish and chose comparative government instead."[40] In the end, Benazir was as happy with her decision as her father. "By studying government at Harvard I began to understand more about Pakistan than I ever had by living there," she explained.

Throughout her years at Harvard, Benazir tried to stay in touch with events at home. In December 1970, Pakistan held its first parliamentary elections in 13 years. "I studied all night by the telephone. When my mother called me to say that my father and the PPP had unexpectedly swept West Pakistan, capturing 82 of 138 seats [from the region] in the National Assembly, I was exultant."[41] Her father was now the leader of the second largest party in the National Assembly; the Awami League of East Pakistan had the most seats, 167 out of a total of 313.

CONFLICT OVER BANGLADESH

Benazir's most difficult year at Harvard may have been 1971. East Pakistan's attempt to secede from Pakistan to form the new nation of Bangladesh strained Benazir's relations with her friends. Peter Galbraith remembered, "Bangladesh provoked the most heated discussions. . . . While the rest of us supported the Bangladeshis, Benazir was the Pakistan patriot, alternately denouncing the secessionists and denying the atrocities. One such argument became so intense that [a friend] . . . literally fled the room into the night."[42] The government-controlled Pakistani press was reporting that the rebellion in East Pakistan had been put down and the region was peaceful, but American papers ran stories of atrocities being committed against

Bhutto learned some of her earliest lessons in politics from American social movements, but her training really began in 1971, when India sent its military to aid in East Pakistan's separation. As Pakistan's foreign minister, Zulfikar Ali Bhutto met with the United Nations in New York to resolve the conflict. Benazir Bhutto became a kind of assistant to him, and in the process she learned firsthand how "power politics" worked. It was the loss of East Pakistan, now Bangladesh, that enabled her father to become Pakistan's president. This photograph shows separatists in Dhaka, Bangladesh, in December 1971.

civilians by the army controlled by West Pakistan. Benazir could not bring herself to believe the Western reports about the rapes and massacres.

By early December, India had intervened in the Pakistan situation militarily. Zulfikar Bhutto, who was foreign minister, flew to the United Nations (UN) in New York to try to convince the Security Council to arrive at a political settlement. He told Benazir to join him there. When she met him, her father asked her if she thought the Security Council would make India withdraw from East Pakistan. Benazir argued that the UN had to intervene because the Indian invasion was clearly illegal. Her father responded, "You may be a good student of international law, Pinkie, and I hesitate to disagree with a Harvard undergraduate. . . . But you don't know anything about power politics."[43]

During the tense days of December 9 to 15, Benazir took notes at meetings and took phone messages from American, Soviet, and Chinese officials for her father. In the midst of the crisis, her father's lessons continued: "Interrupt the meetings," he told her. "If the Soviets are here, tell me the Chinese are calling. If the Americans are here, tell me that the Russians are on the line or the Indians. And don't tell anyone who really is here. One of the fundamental lessons of diplomacy is to create doubt: Never lay all your cards on the table."[44] The situation on the battlefield rapidly deteriorated for West Pakistan, and the permanent members of the Security Council could not agree on a resolution to solve the conflict. After a final, impassioned speech, Zulfikar Bhutto marched out of the chamber in anger. To some, he was making the best of a bad situation and promoting his own political career—he would become prime minister if East Pakistan split off. In Pinkie's eyes, however, her papa was a patriot and a hero.

India defeated Pakistan, taking 93,000 soldiers prisoner and more than 5,000 square miles of territory from West Pakistan. Bangladesh became a new independent country. Pakistani President Mohammed Yahya Khan was forced to resign after the humiliating defeat and handed control of the country to Zulfikar Ali Bhutto, who became the first civilian chief martial law administrator and president. Bhutto, however, could not form a new government and be sworn in as prime minister until a new constitution was written.

Life returned to normal for Benazir after the Bangladesh war ended. According to Peter Galbraith, "Even after her father became president of Pakistan in the middle of her junior year . . . Benazir was able to lead a relatively normal student life. Pakistan seemed very far away."[45] At Harvard, he explained, "She remembered birthdays, baked cakes, and organized social events." Still, Galbraith noted, "Benazir's real passion was for politics," and explained, "At Harvard I knew her as a person of intelligence, assertive and articulate in her opinions, with a rare combination of charm and superb political instinct."[46]

Benazir herself credits the United States with teaching her important political lessons. "I think the most profound influence in my formative years was the years I spent at Harvard. I went there at a time of great social ferment, at a time when the Vietnam war was being fought. . . . I found that if you didn't like something you could do something about it."[47] Benazir was also following the civil rights movement, the labor rights protests of farm workers, and the budding environmental movement as well as the presidential campaign and the women's rights movement. Like her fellow students, she felt it was important to get involved:

> So I was very much into saving the world. My generation grew up in saving the world. We thought education wasn't important. Exams weren't important, although I still did it because I was scared my father would get cross, but I discovered that life was more than my homework and my tuitions and my tutorial. Life was about the larger issues where we could all play a role.[48]

THE SIMLA SUMMIT

When Benazir returned home for summer vacation in 1972, her father continued to expand her political education. He had her accompany him to India, where he would be meeting with Indian Prime Minister Indira Gandhi to negotiate the peace between their two countries. For the first time, Benazir would be traveling on an official visit without her mother and would have to figure out for herself how to act in different situations. On the flight to India, her father told her, "Everyone will be looking for signs of how the meetings are progressing, so be extra careful. . . . You must not smile and give the impression you are enjoying yourself while our soldiers are still in Indian prisoner-of-war camps. You must not look grim, either, which people can interpret as a sign of pessimism."[49] Benazir found these instructions puzzling.

Benazir's clothes were also a worry because most of what she owned was more appropriate for home life or an American college campus than for a visit to another country with a government delegation. Moreover, Benazir explained, "I considered clothes irrelevant. I fancied myself more of a Harvard intellectual whose mind was occupied with the serious questions of war and peace" than with frivolous, material things like clothes.[50]

Benazir borrowed most of the clothes for the trip from a friend and a sari from her mother for more formal occasions. "Even though [my mother] . . . had given me a lesson in wrapping the yards of material securely around me, I was nervous that it would suddenly unravel,"[51] as had once happened to an aunt. To Benazir's embarrassment and surprise, the Indian newspapers wrote her up as a trendsetter in spite of her efforts to downplay any discussion of clothes.

Benazir was given her own schedule to follow while the Indian and Pakistani delegations negotiated. She visited canneries, gardens, and a doll museum and saw dance, gymnastics, and opera performances. The Indian press followed her everywhere.

Almost anything she did seemed newsworthy. The day after she stopped at a bookstore, the UPI headline read "Benazir Goes Shopping, Bystanders Cheer." At times, the crowds of people who followed her blocked the traffic. She was an instant celebrity, receiving letters and telegrams and requests for radio and newspaper interviews.

Benazir did not feel comfortable with all this attention. Neither she nor her father really knew why she was receiving so much coverage. Her father finally speculated that she was the only aspect of the summit meeting the press could cover, because the talks were secret. Benazir came to see more in the situation: "I symbolized a new generation. I had never been an Indian. I had been born in independent Pakistan. I was free of the complexes and prejudices which had torn Indians and Pakistanis apart in the bloody trauma of partition. Perhaps the people were hoping that a new generation could avoid the hostility that had now led to three wars. . . ."[52] Finally, Zulfikar Bhutto and Indira Gandhi hammered out an agreement that brought a peace—though temporary—to the region.

That fall, Benazir returned to Cambridge for her senior year at Harvard. The following spring, she and her friends watched the congressional Watergate hearings, which were investigating a break-in at Democratic Party headquarters by people working for Republican President Richard Nixon. The hearings made a deep impression on her. "The Watergate process left me with a profound sense of the importance of nationally accepted laws, rather than whimsical or arbitrary laws imposed by individuals."[53] The value of a strong constitution had immediate significance for Benazir when, in August 1973, she and her family hopefully watched the National Assembly adopt a new constitution for Pakistan.

Graduation from Harvard was a sad time for Benazir. She liked the Cambridge area and wanted to finish her education in the United States before returning home. Her father, however, wanted her to go to Oxford, in England. "Four years in one place is more than enough, he wrote me. If you stay longer in America, you will begin to put down roots there. It is time for you to move on."[54] In spite of having good friends who would be moving on to Oxford with her, the dutiful daughter strongly chafed at her father's decision. "For the first time I felt my father was pushing me. But what could I do? It was he, after all, who was paying my tuition and expenses. I had no choice. And I was a practical person."[55]

OXFORD DAYS

Zulfikar Bhutto tried to ease Benazir's adjustment to her new life in Oxford. Shortly after her arrival in England, he wrote to her:

> I feel a strange sensation in imagining you walking on the footprints I left behind at Oxford over twenty-two years ago. . . . Your being at Oxford is a dream come true. We pray and hope that this dream turned into reality will grow into a magnificent career in the service of your people.[56]

At first, life at Oxford was lonely and her living conditions felt cramped, lacking in basic conveniences. Benazir found it hard to break through the English reserve to make new friends and had to depend on the Americans she knew from Harvard for companionship. Students could not have telephones in their rooms and instead had to send each other notes through "Oxford's antiquated message system, which generally took two days" to reach the recipient.[57] The food was very plain, without even simple side dishes such as cottage cheese for variety. Her first impression of Oxford was "I have come to a backward place."[58] In the end, though, Benazir was very happy there.

Zulfikar Bhutto believed that Oxford would teach Benazir discipline. "My father had warned me that compared to Harvard, Oxford would teach me to work under pressure. As I struggled to write the required two essays a week for my tutorials in politics, philosophy, and economics, I had to admit he was right."[59] Benazir studied politics, philosophy, and economics for three years. In her fourth year, she studied international law and diplomacy, her chosen career path.

Over time, she joined the Oxford Union debating society, made friends, and began to have a social life. Benazir and her friends went boating, on picnics, and to Stratford-on-Avon to watch Shakespearean plays. They visited London. She gave parties. Her wardrobe expanded because the garden parties she went to during crew season required flowered dresses and hats. She also found herself less unusual at Oxford, which had more Asian students than Radcliffe had.

Her participation in the Oxford Union debating society became an extremely important part of Benazir's life. In her native part of the world, where most people were illiterate, good public speakers were highly valued. She won her first debate at the Oxford Union and continued to be active in the group. After serving on a committee and as treasurer of the Union during her first three years, Benazir ran for president in her fourth year. Her prospects seemed dim. Not only was she a woman in an overwhelmingly male organization, but she was also a foreigner. She had run once before and lost. Not even her father thought she had a chance to win. He wrote to her, "You have to do your best but the result must be accepted in good grace."[60] None of this discouraged her. This time, Benazir won in a surprise victory. Her father's congratulatory telegram read, "OVERJOYED AT YOUR ELECTION AS PRESIDENT OF THE OXFORD UNION. YOU HAVE DONE SPLENDIDLY."[61]

Benazir's lessons in practical politics also continued at Oxford. In February 1974, her father had her fly home to attend a summit he was hosting. The leaders of most Islamic countries attended, and she had the opportunity to meet them.

On the return trip to England, she had a very different experience, unlike any she had ever had. At the airport, a

British customs officer who did not recognize her name examined her papers repeatedly and questioned her sarcastically about her reasons for being in England, finally asking, "How can a Paki have enough money for an Oxford education?"[62] Benazir felt both the personal injustice and the implications of the situation: "I was furious as I turned on my heel and strode out of the airport. If that was how immigration officials were going to treat the daughter of the prime minister, how were they going to treat other Pakistanis, who were not as fluent in English as I was or who were not as aggressive?"[63]

In Pakistan, Zulfikar Ali Bhutto called for elections in the spring of 1977, Benazir's last term at Oxford. The Pakistan People's Party won the majority of the seats in the National Assembly, but it was widely believed that the election was rigged. Antigovernment demonstrations turned into riots, and the Bhutto government suppressed them with violence. The effect of these events reached Benazir in England. "I was startled one afternoon in late March to find a member of Scotland Yard waiting for me. . . . 'I don't wish to alarm you, Miss Bhutto, but there have been reports that you may be in some danger'. . . ."[64] Benazir learned to check her car for bombs and to vary her schedule so she could not be targeted.

PAKISTAN'S GOVERNMENT

The 1973 constitution set up a parliamentary government with two branches: the large National Assembly and the smaller Senate. Members of the National Assembly are directly elected by the people; its leader, the prime minister, is the head of government. That person directs the country's domestic and foreign policy. Senators are elected indirectly by the four provincial assemblies. They vote on bills but do not make policy. The head of state is the president, a figurehead who acts on the advice of the prime minister. The president is elected by the National Assembly and the Senate.

Things remained calm, however, and that June, Benazir gave herself a huge birthday bash to say farewell to England and her friends. Although she was sorry to see the end of her student days, she was eager to return home. Her father had plans for her to work in different sections of government during the summer and early fall until it became time for her to prepare for the Foreign Ministry exams. He had written to her, "I promise you that I will do everything within my capacity to make your readjustment to Pakistan short and pleasant. . . . Both of us will work together for a laudable achievement. You bet we will make it."[65]

4

Thrust Into Politics

1977–1979

It's not a laughing matter. . . . Martial Law is a deadly and dangerous business.

—Zulfikar Ali Bhutto[66]

Benazir Bhutto arrived in Pakistan in the summer of 1977 filled with high hopes and expectations for the future. She immediately set to work with her father. She was put in an office near his and assigned to two projects. One entailed helping the committee that resolved issues between the provincial and federal governments. The second was summarizing and commenting on government reports for her father. In spite of the continuing strikes and protests, 24-year-old Bhutto believed that her father could govern effectively.

Fresh from the West, she held strong democratic values. Moreover, she had tremendous faith in her father's good

34

intentions and ability to solve the country's problems. She was convinced that the 1977 Pakistani elections had been fair. In her eyes, the leaders of the opposition "were not great men or even fine men." She explained,

> They hadn't had the benefit of my father's education, or his extensive experience in government and international diplomacy. In Pakistan, my father was, in fact, unique. . . . Many of those opposing my father were small, provincial men whose myopic views had failed Pakistan in the past and would again in the future."[67]

Benazir also attributed the political upheaval in part to American intervention in Pakistani politics. She believed that the United States wanted to destabilize Zulfikar Bhutto's government and was giving financial support to opposition parties. Over the years, her father had favored many policies that clashed with those of the U.S. government. Other Pakistanis who do not have a favorable view of Zulfikar Bhutto agree that the Americans worked against him.

His supporters also remained faithful. Before taking office, he had promoted socialist reforms to benefit the nation's poor and had spoken out for the rights of peasants and laborers. Once he gained power, his limited land reforms enabled some peasants to obtain small farms and new labor laws gave industrial workers better pensions, health care, and protection from being fired without cause. Bhutto's most significant contribution to the cause of the poor, however, was his recognition of their merit as human beings. Before the advent of the PPP,

> the poor were thought to be good and simple folks as long as they were meek, knew their place, showed deference to the upper . . . classes, and served their

employers and superiors beyond the call of contractual or sanctioned obligation. Bhutto gave them self-respect and a disposition to self-assertion. As a result, they would no longer take abuse or do chores and errands free of charge; they demanded higher wages, rest periods and holidays.[68]

The poor not only supported him, they loved him.

Still, the opposition to his government was more widespread than his daughter could admit. Zulfikar Bhutto earned enemies because of the manner in which some of his reforms were carried out. When the power to determine policy was taken away from the civil service and put in the hands of elected officials, government employees resented the loss and the numerous unneeded workers who were given jobs as a reward for party loyalty. New government industries were built in areas of support for the PPP, and the jobs created became a source of patronage (making appointments to government jobs for political advantage). Corruption among the managers of the new state-run businesses became widespread. Initially, the Bhutto government only national-ized large industries, but the middle class grew concerned as the middle- and small-sized businesses it ran were taken over by the government as well.

Zulfikar Bhutto was an autocrat who concentrated power in his own hands. He did not tolerate opposition either within or outside his party. The more leftist and activist members of the PPP were ousted from the party once it came into power, and the more vocal ones who accused him of betraying the party's principles were put in jail. Bhutto also censored the press. He dismissed the government of Baluchistan when it demanded greater autonomy and sent the army to put down any opposition. In preparation for the 1977 elections, Bhutto had interfered with the ability of opposition parties to run candidates.

Ironically, the PPP had been expected to win the majority of seats in that election, returning Zulfikar Bhutto as prime minister. As a result of the rigged election, the Pakistan National Alliance or PNA, a coalition of parties that had been formed to oppose the PPP, led public protests. Bhutto tried to appease the religious opposition and to suppress the rest to no avail, so he finally entered into negotiations with the PNA. On July 5, two days after they reached an accord agreeing to hold new elections, the army struck.

COUP D'ETAT

Benazir and her siblings were awakened in the middle of the night to news of the coup. A policeman loyal to Zulfikar Bhutto had slipped into the prime minister's residence in Rawalpindi to warn him. The children ran to their parents' bedroom, where they found their father on the phone, learning of other government officials who had been arrested. He soon found that General Mohammed Zia ul-Haq, his army chief of staff, had led the coup. The general told Bhutto that he would be placed in protective custody at the prime minister's rest house for 90 days until elections were held. He would be picked up at 2:30 A.M. When he hung up, the Bhuttos' last phone line went dead. An angry Mir wanted to resist the coup in some way, but his father told him, "Never resist a military coup. The generals want us dead. We must give them no pretext to justify our murders."[69]

As the family waited anxiously, 2:30 went by and no one came to get Mr. Bhutto. As the hours dragged on, Bhutto noted, "They hadn't even prepared the rest house. They'd made plans for the arrests of . . . [other government officials], but not for me."[70] With sudden realization, Shah Nawaz said to Benazir, "The bastard was planning to murder us in our beds."[71] To Nusrat Bhutto's relief, the boys were allowed to leave a short time later. Some time after 8:00 in the morning, Zulfikar Bhutto was taken away.

For three weeks, the family was separated. Zulfikar Bhutto issued directions by telephone that the rest of the family carried out. Mir was sent to Larkana to meet with supporters in the Bhuttos' home district and Benazir and Shah were set to work in Karachi and Lahore. Because General Zia had announced that elections would be held on October 18, there was much to do to prepare for the campaign. Benazir, whose ability to speak Urdu, the official language of Pakistan, had become rusty during her years in the West, worked with a tutor every day so she could give speeches and talk with party workers.

Even after Bhutto's release, the family remained uneasy. He received several warnings from friends with connections to General Zia that he would be arrested soon and that the army was looking for charges for which he could be given the death sentence. Still, he refused to leave Pakistan.

Shortly before dawn on September 3, Benazir was startled when six army commandos burst into her bedroom. While five pointed guns at her, the sixth threw her clothes, books, and other possessions to the floor. When they left and she made her way to her parents' room, Benazir found commandos all over the house. Her initial fear had changed to defiance, and she said to Sanam, "Look at these soldiers. . . . How can they be so *besharam,* so shameless. It was their prime minister, Zulfikar Ali Bhutto, who brought them back from the camps of India where their generals had left them to rot. And this is how they repay him, by entering his home and violating its sanctity?" [72]

There was nothing Benazir could do. The former prime minister was taken away, and Nusrat Bhutto, Shah Nawaz, the girls, and the servants were held without means of communication for the rest of the day. Benazir began to see martial law at work. Although the judge who heard the accusations against Zulfikar Bhutto dismissed the case and released him after ten days, he was arrested again five days later and was never released again. The three younger children were sent back to school overseas, although the boys soon dropped out to work on obtaining foreign support for their father's freedom. Benazir chose to stay at home.

While her husband was in prison, Nusrat Bhutto was elected acting chair of the Pakistan People's Party. She traveled around the country campaigning for the upcoming elections. Benazir reluctantly went as well. "Standing on the makeshift stage in the industrial city of Faisalabad, I was terrified. At twenty-four years, I did not think of myself yet as a political leader or a public speaker. But I had no choice."[73] Soon, Benazir was addressing large public rallies and small groups. At the third city of her campaign tour, she was placed under house arrest. The next day, General Zia postponed the elections. Meanwhile, Benazir was held for two weeks, unable to use the telephone and, at times, without water or electricity.

NUSRAT BHUTTO

Nusrat Bhutto set an example of leadership and activism for her children. She had been an involved first lady, always at her husband's side. She led the Pakistani delegation to Mexico City for the United Nations Conference on Women in 1975 and was elected vice president of the event. She was called *begum,* a title of respect.

Begum Bhutto defied the martial law authorities many times. She led demonstrations to free her husband when he was imprisoned by President Mohammed Ayub Khan. When Zulfikar Ali Bhutto was on trial, she accepted the chairmanship of the Pakistan People's Party despite debilitating illness. She traveled the country, delivering rousing speeches to her husband's supporters and bringing aid to party loyalists who needed it. After his death, she continued to work as a leader of her party and the opposition against Zia and spent long periods in jail. After the return of civilian government in 1988, she was elected to the National Assembly for five terms. She also served as cabinet minister during her daughter's first term as prime minister.

ZULFIKAR BHUTTO ON TRIAL

Zulfikar Bhutto's trial began in late October and lasted five months. He was accused of having ordered the murder of a member of the National Assembly who opposed many of his policies. Benazir and her mother rented a house in Lahore, where the trial was held. Throughout the trial, Zulfikar instructed his wife and daughter on how to prepare his defense and how to keep their supporters in spirits. Numerous other charges of corruption were brought against him, and Benazir was kept busy going through family records to find evidence to disprove them. She met regularly with her father's attorneys and helped put together responses to the charges that were distributed to the press. She visited supporters, especially those who were suffering under martial law, and spoke with the party faithful. Nevertheless, in March 1978, Zulfikar Bhutto was found guilty and sentenced to death.

During his trial, Bhutto was kept in a primitive cell with little running water and a dirt floor, next to mentally ill prisoners who made noise during the night, keeping him awake. He was also forced to listen to the cries of other prisoners who were being punished physically. After his conviction, he was held in continually worsening conditions. He was moved to a dark, damp, mosquito-ridden cell with no toilet. In another cell, he had a metal bed frame without a mattress, and in his last cell, only a roll of bedding on the floor.

In the year that followed, Zulfikar Bhutto suffered from dysentery, malaria, influenza, and gum disease. He was denied medical attention, yet his spirit did not falter, and Benazir derived strength from his example. She not only loved him but also admired his courage, pride, and determination and his insistence in maintaining his personal dignity. He, however, maintained no false hopes. When Benazir visited him one day full of hope and optimism because the evidence against him was not holding up, he tried to get her to face reality. "You don't understand, do you, Pinkie," he answered. "They are going to kill me. It doesn't matter what evidence you or anyone comes up with." [74] For Benazir, this message was too difficult to take in. "My father tried to tell me what lay ahead. But I heard his words as if from a great distance. And I kept them there. Otherwise, I could not have gone on to fight the one new charge after another being brought against him. The fight to save his honor became my own." [75]

Meanwhile, Benazir and her mother were subjected to house arrests and harassment. Family pride, loyalty, and courage helped Benazir and her mother continue fighting, even though their health suffered. Benazir developed a middle ear problem that required surgery. It became acute during the three-month detention she was given when her father was condemned, but the government denied her proper medical care. She finally had surgery after her release. Through the months of legal wrangling, detention, and anxiety, she lost a great deal of weight and developed acne and insomnia. Nusrat Bhutto, who had a history of low blood pressure, needed medication for her condition on repeated occasions. Nonetheless, mother and daughter carried on.

Zulfikar Bhutto saw little point in appealing his verdict to the Supreme Court, but when the Bhutto women insisted, he acquiesced. The second trial was held in Rawalpindi. Once again, Benazir became involved in her father's defense. She spoke with foreign reporters—because Pakistani newspapers were under government control—and a friend typed and retyped the legal papers for her father's defense. Once again, her father sent Benazir on a political tour around Pakistan. During her visits to him, he coached her on what to say to people in different regions and how to present herself.

Benazir was back in detention during her father's appeal. Her mother told her how he had spoken eloquently in his own defense, but, in the end, the Supreme Court upheld the death sentence by a controversial four to three vote. The Supreme Court recommended that the sentence be commuted to life in

Benazir Bhutto emerged from her studies in the United States and Great Britain with a belief in democratic values. Soon after her return to Pakistan, though, she saw the harsher realities of Pakistani politics. Her father was overthrown in 1977, and during his two years in prison his family toured the country to speak on his behalf. Benazir traveled and spoke, too, despite her discomfort—but all their efforts were in vain. When her father was executed, Bhutto resolved to continue his work for a more democratic Pakistan.

prison, and foreign leaders sent numerous appeals for mercy to General Zia, raising Benazir's hopes. Zia refused. Zulfikar Ali Bhutto was executed on April 4, 1979. By that time, he was emaciated from the maltreatment, disease, and hunger strikes he had gone on in protest. Still, he insisted on bathing and changing into clean clothes beforehand to die on his own terms.

Zulfikar Bhutto understood all along what Benazir had not wanted to hear. In the hard world of Pakistani politics, General Zia had to execute him to ensure his own survival. The general's coup was treason according to the Pakistani constitution, and the punishment for treason was death. If Bhutto had been allowed to resume his position as prime minister, Zia would have been convicted and executed.

Zulfikar Bhutto's death dramatically changed the lives of the rest of his family. For Benazir, her father's death forced her to face a profound "feeling of helplessness." Years later, she said, "I knew that morning that he was going to be killed, but there was nothing—nothing—I could do. . . . [T]hat comes back to haunt me, over and over again."[76] During her last visit with her father, the day before his death, she gave up her dream of being a diplomat and committed herself to politics, the career he had selected for her from the start. When her father suggested that she leave Pakistan and return to Europe or the United States to live in peace, she responded, "No, papa, I will continue the struggle that you began for democracy."[77]

5

Imprisonment and Exile

1979–1987

I will neither leave the scene nor allow anyone else to rise.
—General Mohammed Zia ul-Haq[78]

Benazir and Begum Nusrat Bhutto were placed under house arrest at Al-Murtaza toward the end of 1979. After their release the following April, they attempted to resume their political activities but also had to attend to personal matters. Benazir's middle ear infection had flared up again but had not been given adequate medical treatment. When her eardrum burst after a flight to Rawalpindi to meet with supporters, she had to be rushed to the hospital. After she rejoined her mother in Karachi, Benazir requested permission to travel abroad for treatment, but her letter was ignored.

The Bhutto women were not ignored by the Zia government, however. Their phones were tapped, they were watched by intelligence agents, and their visitors were photographed and had their license plates registered. Nusrat Bhutto asked Benazir to return to Al-Murtaza to go over the family finances, check on the farms that had been neglected for the past two years, and make improvements to the house—where her mother suspected they might be detained again. Benazir felt awkward because the lands and the tenants had always been her father and brothers' concern, but she did as her mother requested.

Begum Bhutto had good reason for her suspicions. Under martial law, military courts with the power to try and punish civilians were established. The press was censored, and it became illegal to express opinions against the government. About 20,000 political opponents were arrested between 1978 and 1985.[79] Many prisoners were flogged; others were tortured. International human rights organizations documented numerous cases of abuse. Labor protests were prohibited, and the army put down strikes demanding higher pay or benefits.

Corruption and drug smuggling became serious concerns, and drug addiction became a problem in Pakistan for the first time. Through a policy of "Islamization," General Zia also introduced punishments such as amputation of a hand or foot for theft, flogging for drinking alcohol, and stoning to death for adultery. In the end, none of these punishments was ever carried out, but the threat was regularly used to harass people. Women also lost many of their rights. Their testimony was worth half of a man's in legal cases, and restrictions were placed upon them regarding financial dealings.

In 1978, the general named himself president. After he cancelled the 1979 elections, the Pakistan National Alliance, which had opposed the Pakistan People's Party, asked the PPP to join it in the fight to oust Zia. Various PPP leaders, including Benazir, wanted nothing to do with the people who had helped bring about Zulfikar Bhutto's downfall, but Begum Bhutto believed that the groups should work together to reestablish democracy first and then let the voters choose between them. Her views prevailed, and the Movement for the Restoration of Democracy (MRD) was formed in February 1981. When the MRD staged demonstrations and strikes, the Zia regime struck back. Thousands of people were arrested, and many were beaten, kept awake for days, and tortured with electric wires and other means.

Fully expecting to be arrested, Nusrat Bhutto had instructed her daughter not to participate in any political

MOHAMMED ZIA UL-HAQ

General Zia ul-Haq was originally from what is now India. He served in the British Army during World War II, and, after the partition of India, joined the Pakistani army. He took a course at the Commander and Staff College of the United States from 1963 to 1964 and served in Pakistan's 1965 war with India. He served in other postings and rose in rank. In 1976, Prime Minister Bhutto passed over five other generals to name Zia chief of army staff. Bhutto expected Zia to be loyal to him as his benefactor.

Scholars disagree as to the depth of Zia's personal commitment to Islam, but his Islamization policy even guided his economic policy. He introduced Islamic banking, which did not permit the charging or earning of interest, putting Pakistan at odds with financial practices in the developed world and the financial institutions from which Pakistan needed to borrow money. A soldier to the end, after he assumed the presidency, General Zia continued to live in the house of the chief of army staff rather than as a civilian in the president's house. He once told a reporter, "I've discovered that gaining power is much easier than giving it up."*

* Weaver, *Pakistan*, 58.

activities for the time being. She wanted Benazir to remain free to lead the party after her own detention. Benazir was even sent away from 70 Clifton when meetings were held there. Meanwhile, Mir Murtaza and Shah Nawaz had formed their own resistance group abroad called Al-Zulfikar. On March 2, a member of Al-Zulfikar hijacked a Pakistan International Airlines plane and forced it to land in Kabul, where the brothers gave the hijacker a warm welcome. The government tried to link Al-Zulfikar with the PPP and arrested many members of the party. Within days, Begum and Benazir Bhutto were taken to prison while the government worked to connect them to the hijacking. For Benazir, the hijacking was "an awful mistake" and a serious setback to the movement to oust Zia.[80]

SUKKUR JAIL

About 200 PPP women were taken to Sukkur prison. While there, the women

> scrubbed the prison's floors and disinfected their cells; killed mosquitoes, flies, and rats; worked in the kitchen; did the laundry; or stitched and repaired their jailers' uniforms. . . . [One of Benazir's aides] often spent five or six hours a day washing a hundred or so uniforms by hand, beating them against rocks, then ironing them on a cracked concrete floor.[81]

Sukkur jail is in the Sindhi desert, where temperatures climb to 120 degrees. Another of Benazir's aides described their situation in Sukkur jail: "We were held in crumbling barracks . . . or, sometimes, in tiny cells with no windows—no ventilation—and it was unearthly hot."[82]

Although Benazir was also taken to Sukkur jail, the other women never saw her. She was kept in isolation in a cell without walls, only iron bars all around. It had no toilet or sink; she was given pails of yellowish-brown water for drinking and washing. The only furniture was the cot she slept on, and the single light bulb in the ceiling was turned off at 7:00 P.M. Benazir recalled, "The winds blew constantly through the open sides of my cell. . . . A constant dust storm swirled in my cell. Sticky with sweat, I was often coated with grit." She continued, "My skin split and peeled, coming off my hands in sheets. More boils erupted on my face. The sweat dripped into them, burning like acid. My hair, which had always been thick, began to come out by the handful."[83]

She was also subjected to a steady barrage of pests: "Grasshoppers. Mosquitoes. Stinging flies. Bees. . . . Big black ants. Cockroaches. Seething clumps of little red ants. Spiders. I tried pulling the sheet over my head at night to hide from their bites, pushing it back when it got too hot to breathe."[84] When she asked her jailers for insect spray, Benazir was told she could not have it because she might use it to commit suicide. The superintendent of the prison raised the suggestion that she might commit suicide when he visited her every week, and a bottle of poisonous detergent was regularly left in her cell.

Benazir was also denied proper medical attention for a gynecological problem. When her condition worsened after about a month of imprisonment, she was rushed off to a hospital in Karachi, where she had surgery—without ever being told what the surgery was for. Then she was returned to her cell at Sukkur before she could stand up by herself.

Benazir suffered mental punishment as well as. She was allowed one newspaper each day but was denied other reading material that might help her pass the time. At one point, she was told that death cells were being prepared for her in another part of Sukkur prison because she was going to be tried by a military court and sentenced to death. She heard a rumor that she was going to be transferred to a torture center, where she would be forced to confess how she was involved in the hijacking, and she was told that all the other PPP members were defecting and joining Zia and was advised to give up politics.

When her first detention order ended in June, Benazir was given a second one. This order was for a class A cell, entitling her to a radio, television, refrigerator, and air-conditioning. The only privilege the superintendent actually offered her was that of walking about the courtyard at night. Benazir stuck to her principles and wrote back to him, "I decline your 'A' class status. . . . I will not be party to your lies."[85]

Benazir held on to her principles and her self-respect for the six long months she was at Sukkur jail. She passed the lonely hours exercising and working on some embroidery the jailers allowed her to do. She read her newspaper as slowly as possible, ignoring the stories about her mother and her, and gleaning as much information as she could from the censored articles. She kept a journal in which she wrote her thoughts about the significance of events in other countries. She also wrote down personal thoughts: "Each hour has passed more slowly than a day or a week and yet I have come so far."[86] And she analyzed her situation: "'Adjusted' is not the right word. I cannot adjust to a situation which is abhorrent. To adjust is to give in. I have coped. Each moment has dragged, but it has also passed. God alone has helped me in this ordeal. Without Him, I would have perished."[87] Contemplating the possibility of being tried and executed, she wrote, "Death comes in the end and I do not fear it. . . . The animals in the regime can only eliminate people. They cannot eliminate concepts. The concept of democracy will survive. And in the inevitable victory of democracy, we will live again."[88] Her guards hid the notebook at night in case the senior staff conducted a surprise inspection.

One of the matrons guarding her taught Benazir a prayer that was supposed to get her released after four weeks. The prayer, "Say He Is One God," is a verse from the Koran. "I started . . . reciting the verse forty-one times. . . . I prayed for every prisoner. I prayed for my mother. I prayed for myself."[89] Four weeks later, Benazir was taken to visit her mother, who was being held in Karachi Central Jail. When she was returned to Sukkur, Benazir continued praying. After another four weeks, Begum Bhutto—who was very ill—was released from prison. Encouraged, Benazir prayed harder. Several weeks later, on August 15, she was transferred to the cell in which her mother had been held in Karachi.

To her dismay, Benazir found herself in isolation again. Although her cell was indoors, the toilet did not work and her water pail was covered with dead insects. The electricity was cut off for several hours each day. At least she was allowed to have the food that her mother sent and she was near her family. Benazir's health continued to deteriorate, but her spirits lifted a little at the thought that she might be released September 13, when her detention order was supposed to end. She resumed her exercise and prayers and hoped that she might be released for her sister's wedding on the eighth. She was allowed to attend two happy days of family celebrations, but she was taken back to prison the day after the wedding. On the thirteenth, she was served with a detention notice for another three months.

During her time in Karachi Central Jail, various psychological tricks were played on Benazir to unsettle her and convince her to sign a paper renouncing future political activities. Every week, the prison superintendent would assure her that she could be free the next day if she would just sign the paper. Benazir was troubled by his kind manner and suspicious of his words: "I knew the superintendent would never dare say such things without official support.

After supplanting Zulfikar Ali Bhutto as president of Pakistan, General Zia ul-Haq (shown here in 1986) persecuted and imprisoned members of the Bhutto family. While Benazir and her mother endured their imprisonment, groups in Pakistan and the United States lobbied for their release. Benazir Bhutto was finally freed in 1984, after five years in abysmal conditions. She returned to London, gathered allies, and began working to remove Zia from power. She spoke eloquently against his human rights violations until his sudden death four years later.

Yet if Zia wanted to free me, he would. If he didn't, he wouldn't. But what was the point of trying to blackmail me, to compromise me? Did they really think I would consent?

Or were they just trying to break me. . . ?"[90] The jailers used other tactics to unsettle her, too. Sometimes Benazir would hear voices or footsteps or other noises outside her cell during the night, but when she complained, she was told she was imagining them. Finally, the superintendent suggested that, because her cell block had been built over an old hanging ground, the sounds might come from a restless soul. Others on the jail staff tried to be kind to her when they could.

ALONE UNDER HOUSE ARREST

Finally, at the end of 1981, Benazir was transferred to house arrest in Al-Murtaza. For almost a year, she was under guard and very much alone. Each time a three-month detention order ended, she was served with a new one, and eventually she stopped thinking that she might be released. Her phone calls were monitored, and her only news came from state-controlled television. Family visits were rare: It was difficult for Sanam to get away from her responsibilities, and Begum Bhutto was too sick to travel. Whenever Benazir realized that she was feeling sorry for herself, she would feel guilty and remind herself that she was fortunate to be in her home, where she had food, clean water, and clothes. As she had done during her first winter at Harvard, she found something useful to do: She took out her mother's cookbooks and, following the recipes, learned to cook. "Every dish I produced then—curries, rice, *dahl* [a dish made of pureed or spiced legumes]—became a mini-triumph of sorts. . . . I could look at a bowl of rice I'd made and see in it proof that I existed. . . . I cook, therefore I am."[91] In November 1982, she was taken to Karachi to see her mother before Begum Bhutto—seriously ill with cancer—was finally allowed to leave Pakistan.

What Benazir hoped for but did not know during the years in solitary confinement was that their friends had not forgotten them. Supporters both at home and abroad had pressed for Begum Bhutto's permit to travel, and the women of Sindh had staged a demonstration for her. In England, where many of the Pakistanis who had fled Zia's repression settled, old friends from Pakistan and Oxford, together with human rights organizations, obtained the support of several members of Parliament, who made public pleas for her release. In the United States, Benazir's old friend Peter Galbraith had aroused the concern of his boss, Senator Claiborne Pell of Rhode Island, who served on the Foreign Relations Committee. Senator John Glenn of Ohio, the former astronaut, wrote to the Pakistani ambassador to the United States requesting that she be allowed to travel.

The American senators' interest had a direct effect on Benazir's situation. Pakistan was receiving monetary aid from the United States for its role in the war in Afghanistan against the Soviets. A number of senators had doubts about granting aid to a regime with a record of human rights abuses. These objections prompted her move from Karachi Central Jail to Al-Murtaza.

After her mother's departure for Europe, Benazir's detention at 70 Clifton continued, but she managed to resume political activities. The servants smuggled her instructions to party workers, evading the eyes of the agents who followed them around the city whenever they ran errands. When she read in the paper that local elected officials planned to meet with Zia when the general visited Sindh, she sent word that doing so was against party policy. Some of the officials met with Zia anyway, and, knowing that she was taking a risk, Benazir called one of the party heads and directed him to expel them. After that, her phone was permanently cut off, all visitors were prohibited, and searches of her servants intensified. Benazir carried on. When the MRD called for agitation to protest the government-controlled elections Zia had announced would take place by 1985, she helped organize and fund it.

Benazir developed various health problems during the years in detention. The doctors and dentists the regime sent told her she was imagining her ailments or did not provide appropriate care. The middle ear problem grew so bad that she became dizzy, heard clicking noises in her head, and lost some hearing. One day she became so dizzy that she fainted. Instead of the usual government doctors who would not see her for days, a local doctor was quickly called in and referred her to an ear specialist. The specialist began to treat her and advised her to get permission to go abroad for microscopic surgery. He added, "I can do [an] . . . operation here, but I'm frightened they'll put pressure on me to do something under the anesthesia. . . . Even if I refuse, they'll get somebody else to do it. On all counts, it's much better for you to go abroad." [92]

The doctor was threatened by the regime, but he continued to treat Benazir and stabilized her condition. She applied for permission to go abroad, torn between staying in Pakistan, where thousands were living in jail under worse conditions than she was, and leaving to regain her health. Finally, in December 1983, she and Sanam were told to prepare to travel.

Meanwhile, in the United States, Senator Pell continued pressing the Pakistani government about Benazir's situation. The Foreign Relations Committee sent Peter Galbraith to Pakistan in early January 1984 to meet with her. He arrived in Karachi on the ninth, ready to test General Zia's statements to the senators that she was allowed to have visitors and lived comfortably. Galbraith explained, "For the Pakistan authorities, there could be no good outcome: either I saw Benazir and included in my official report an account of her confinement, or they denied me permission to see her—in which case Zia's unkept promises could be used to embarrass him publicly."[93] Galbraith never saw her. In the early hours of January 10, Benazir and Sanam were put on a plane for Geneva, Switzerland.

RETURN TO EUROPE

In Geneva, Benazir was reunited with her mother and brother Mir and met his 18-month-old daughter, Fathi, for the first time. From there, Benazir and Sanam flew to London, where she stayed at her aunt's apartment, for the surgery. She later recounted,

> For all that I was free, I dreaded going out of the flat. Every time I stepped out the front door my stomach, my neck, and my shoulders tensed. I couldn't walk two steps without turning around to see if I was being followed. After all the years of living alone behind prison walls, even the crowded streets in London seemed threatening. I wasn't used to people, to voices, to noise.[94]

Benazir had the surgery at the end of January and then recuperated under her mother's care. Although she had hoped to return to Pakistan soon, she had to change her plans when she learned that she might need a second operation in nine months to a year. Friends and relatives suggested that in the meantime she stay in the West and lead a normal life. Benazir, however, decided to resume political work in England, where 378,000 Pakistanis lived.

Benazir decided to fight Zia by bringing his human rights violations to international attention. She began gathering information about different political prisoners; once well enough to travel, she set off her campaign with a visit to the United States. There, she met with the various senators who had supported her during her imprisonment, made a speech at the Carnegie Endowment for International Peace in Washington, and gave an interview to the editors of *Time* magazine in New York, one of whom was a Harvard classmate. She was nervous, but she pressed on. On her return to London, she took an apartment in a "fortress-like" building where she felt safe from Pakistani agents and gathered a group of volunteers for her campaign. Her spare bedroom served as their office.

They lobbied foreign governments and the secretary-general of the United Nations, organized letter-writing campaigns to save prisoners who were likely to receive death sentences, met with human rights groups, and got the support of labor leaders who publicized the way workers were being mistreated. To document the human rights abuses, they had prisoners secretly fill out questionnaires that were smuggled out of Pakistan. The group began printing a monthly magazine called *Amal,* meaning "action." *Amal* was smuggled into Pakistan, where it was passed on to the PPP faithful and prisoners. Benazir spoke to Pakistani community groups and lobbied European politicians.

When President Zia finally announced that "non-party" national elections would be held in early 1985, the MRD decided to boycott. Although the idea of a parliamentary system without ruling and opposition parties was absurd, Bhutto was not happy with the MRD decision. "Never leave a field open, my father had said over and over." [95] She believed that it would have been better to offer candidates who would oppose the government. Publicly, though, she supported the MRD position. The election took place as planned, and the great majority of those elected were traditional leaders, such as feudal lords and tribal heads. With the new National Assembly, the constitution would again be in force, but Zia kept all the power in his own hands by declaring a series of amendments that gave the president ultimate authority over all decisions and the power to dismiss the National Assembly. He appointed Mohammed Khan Junejo as prime minister.

In July, Benazir took time off from politics to go to a family reunion on the French Riviera. She was looking forward to more than a week of beach and family fun. Within days, however, Shah Nawaz was discovered dead from poisoning in his apartment. His wife, who had been home with him, had not called the police or an ambulance. Many Bhutto supporters believed that he had been murdered. Benazir and Sanam took his body back to Larkana for burial in the family burial ground, and when they got off the plane in Mohenjo-Daro, more than a million people were waiting for them to pay their respects. For many Sindhis, Shah Nawaz had become *shaheed*, a martyr. Benazir was put under house arrest when she returned to Karachi at the end of August. She was released two months later when a French court asked her to give a deposition regarding her brother's death.

COMING HOME

Benazir decided to return to Pakistan in 1986. In preparation, she flew to Washington, D.C., to meet with her supporters in Congress. She also traveled to the Soviet Union to speak before a women's organization. Benazir wanted to show that she had international support and also to not appear too pro-American to the leftist members of her own party. Having received a number of death threats, she felt that she needed to make personal preparations. To fulfill a promise she had made to her father, Benazir went to Mecca on a religious pilgrimage called the Umrah. Unlike those of the Hajj, the rituals of the Umrah require only a few hours to complete, and the pilgrim can go any time during the year. She prayed for her father, her brother, and others who suffered. "I felt my burdens lighten as we performed the rituals of the Umrah. . . . I felt uplifted by the religious experience, and stayed an extra day to perform the Umrah a second time for myself." [96]

Prime Minister Junejo had eased many of the martial law restrictions, such as total censorship of the press and the ban on political parties, and he allowed Benazir to return in April 1986. Three million people went to greet her in Lahore, her first stop. A friend remembered the excitement caused by her return:

> The sight of Lahore the night before Benazir's arrival was like that of a giant carnival or festival. . . . Camps were set up all over the city with food and drink. . . . The whole city was in the hands of the people. Students in Suzuki vans were moving through the streets, singing songs about the Bhuttos. . . . People kept arriving in cars, in buses, in bullock carts, in trucks, by foot. I saw a whole caravan of buses jammed with people, waving banners. . . .
>
> No one slept the whole night. We walked around the city and back and forth to the airport along with everyone else. One old man walked with us for a way, tears in his eyes. Another old lady joined us, crying bitterly at times, then smiling. No one had been able to grieve for Mr. Bhutto. There had been no formal mourning period. Now people were finally able to express their grief as well as their joy over Benazir's return. Lahore that night was one of the most beautiful experiences of my life.[97]

For the first time, Benazir saw how many people were affected by the commitment she had made to her father to continue his work. She recalled that as she was about to leave the airport:

> I gripped the notes for my speech as I looked at the rickety stairs leading to the platform which had been built on the top of the truck for me to ride on. I sometimes

had nightmares of a stairway I didn't want to climb, but had to. Suddenly that very stairway was in front of me and hundreds of expectant eyes were waiting to watch me climb it. . . . I put my foot on the first step and took a deep breath. '*Bismallah*,' I said to myself. 'In the name of God, I begin.'" [98]

Benazir toured through Punjab and then went west to the Frontier Province and south to Baluchistan before arriving home in Karachi. Huge crowds met her everywhere. In May, she was elected cochair (with Begum Bhutto) of the PPP. On August 14, Pakistan Independence Day, the government cracked down on the opposition. At MRD rallies in Lahore and Karachi, people were sprayed with tear gas and beaten by the police. Later that day, Benazir was arrested while giving a press conference and put in solitary confinement. Protests in Pakistan and pressure from abroad won her release the following month.

PAKISTAN'S BRIDE

The following year, 1987, her mother and aunt finally persuaded Benazir to think about getting married. As a Muslim woman who spent most of the day surrounded by men, her reputation needed to be protected. Her parents had first discussed the possibility of marriage with her when she returned to Pakistan in 1977, but for several years, the question had been irrelevant to Benazir. While her father was imprisoned, she had no interest in the subject, and, when he was executed, she decided not to marry for two years. By the time the two years were up, she was in prison. After her release, she needed to recover both physically and emotionally, and then, just as she was feeling more like herself, Shah Nawaz was murdered.

In 1987, Benazir's relatives mounted a campaign to get her married. Not having met a man she wanted to marry, an arranged match was now her only option. Her father's sister had been approached by a landed family from Sindh who had an only son, Asif Ali Zardari. Zardari would inherit extensive lands and become the head of a large tribe. After deciding he was a suitable candidate, Benazir's aunt passed the offer on to Nusrat Bhutto, who also approved. When the offer was finally brought to Benazir, she began to reconsider her private life. With most of her family in Europe, she was often lonely at 70 Clifton, and, at age 34, she was ready to have a family. Nevertheless, she had serious doubts.

Benazir flew to London in July for a week of marriage negotiations. She tried to raise all the problems a man married to a woman in her position would face. She would travel frequently, attend meetings that ran late into the night, and have very little time for relaxation and social life. Most important for a Muslim family, she would have to break with the tradition of living with her in-laws because she would need a house in which she could run political meetings. Also, Zardari had a reputation as a playboy, and she had to be sure he was ready to settle down because any indiscretion on his part would reflect on her. Benazir did not want to rush her decision. Once she agreed to a marriage, it would have to be permanent. Even if the marriage were unhappy, in order to preserve her public career, she could not get a divorce.

In the end, she found that she liked Zardari's sense of humor and felt that both of them were prepared to bring commitment, "good will and respect" to the marriage.[99] Another factor also influenced her decision. As Benazir put it, "Fate presented itself in the form of a bee" that stung her. When Zardari discovered her swollen hand, he took control. "He ignored my protests, calling for a car, arranging for the doctor, buying the prescribed medicine. For once I am not the one in charge, I thought. I am the one being cared for. It was a very nice and unaccustomed feeling."[100]

Benazir Bhutto married Asif Zardari on December 17, 1987. Two receptions were held: one for family, friends, and dignitaries from around the world and a second, the "people's" reception, for PPP supporters, at a sports field in Lyari, a poor neighborhood of Karachi. Fifteen thousand invitations were sent out for the people's reception; more than 200,000 people attended.

6

Mohtarma
1987–1993

Miss Bhutto is not the problem. . . . It is Miss Bhutto's unnecessary, impractical ambitions and her attitude towards acquiring power which is objectionable.

—General Mohammed Zia ul-Haq [101]

All through 1987, Benazir Bhutto traveled around Pakistan. She condemned Zia's abuse of basic rights and the corruption of his regime. She also pursued her contacts abroad. The fact that she could influence public opinion, however, did not mean that she could oust the general. In 1988, unexpected events changed the situation in Pakistan. Prime Minister Junejo had been at odds with General Zia for some time. In May of that year, using the powers he had given himself under the Eighth Amendment to the constitution, Zia dismissed Junejo and the entire National Assembly. Because the country was now governed by the constitution and not martial law, the general was forced to call for new elections. He again called for partyless elections. Bhutto convinced the MRD to take part in these elections in spite of Zia's restrictions and began to prepare.

Bhutto was now in charge of running her first campaign, and she prepared to run more than one kind of campaign. In past elections, the symbol of each candidate's party was placed on the ballot next to the person's name. This helped the voting public, most of which was illiterate, identify the candidates who supported the policies they liked. In partyless elections, candidates would have no symbol next to their names, so the PPP filed a petition before the Supreme Court asking that partyless elections be declared unconstitutional. Bhutto hoped that the court would rule in their favor, but in the meantime, she prepared for partyless elections by getting as many people with well-known names to run as was possible. Among them was Nusrat Bhutto, who agreed to return to Pakistan and politics.

An unexpected event, however, changed the political situation even more radically. On August 17, the plane carrying General Zia crashed. The general, along with everyone else on board, was killed. When she heard the news, Bhutto's first reaction was relief: "I felt an enormous burden lift from my shoulders. After eleven years of torture and harassment, we were free. And he was gone. Zia could never hurt us again." [102] The cause of the crash was never found, and Bhutto came to the conclusion that the general's death was God's punishment for what he had done to the country and her father.

After Zia's death, General Mirza Aslam Beg became the chief of staff of the army. He and other top officers decided to permit the elections to go through as planned and not declare another period of martial law. In October, the Supreme Court declared political parties constitutional. Candidates would be able to have symbols next to their names. The MRD was the group most likely to win enough seats to form a government in the National Assembly, but the PPP and the other groups in the

After her marriage to Asif Ali Zardari in 1987 and General Zia ul-Haq's death in 1988, Bhutto moved aggressively into Pakistani politics. She adopted the title of *Mohtarma* ("Esteemed Lady") to counteract Pakistani prejudice against female politicians, and she managed to become prime minister in December 1988. But the victory was short-lived; after only two years in office, she was accused of corruption and removed from power. This photograph shows Zardari and Bhutto in court in 1990. Zardari was convicted in September, but the charges stood for less than a month.

MRD could not agree on candidates or on the way to share power after the elections. The two groups separated, and Bhutto turned her attention to selecting PPP candidates for the

National and provincial assemblies. At the same time, the army and the caretaker government created obstacles for the opposition parties. They wanted to make sure that no party could get a majority, because a majority would allow it to challenge the army's power or take away the benefits that Zia's civilian cronies enjoyed.

A POLITICAL NEWBORN

As the elections approached, Bhutto was well into her first pregnancy. She had felt healthy and strong for most of the summer, able to work 15 or more hours every day. At the end of August, however, she was forced to pay more attention to herself and the baby. With two months to go before her due date, the doctor found that the baby did not have enough amniotic fluid and was not getting enough nourishment. Bhutto was immediately put on bed rest for four days and told to lie down for an hour every morning and evening after that; she was not to discuss politics while resting but to concentrate on feeling the baby. She was also instructed to get a fetal stress test every four days and to be ready to go to the hospital for a caesarean section at any moment.

For three more weeks, Bhutto continued working long hours. She and her husband slipped out at night to go to the clinic for the stress tests. They also moved from 70 Clifton to their own house. Bhutto's own stress level mounted. Finally, on September 21, Bhutto had her son by caesarean section. The baby was small but healthy. She and Zardari named him Bilawal, "one without equal."[103] They also named their new home Bilawal House, after him.

Politics were never far from Bhutto's private life, and the connection people felt with the Bhuttos carried over into that life. Before she arrived at the hospital for the birth, word had spread that she was on her way and crowds began to gather outside—even though no announcement had been made. Her choice of a hospital had been in part political—to declare her solidarity with the poor who supported the PPP and to set an example for them. She gave birth at a hospital in Lyari, the neighborhood in which she and Zardari had had their people's reception.

The government had forbidden candidates from advertising on radio and television, so, after a short period recuperating from the birth and a subsequent kidney infection, Bhutto was forced to go on the campaign trail. She traveled by train through the Punjab, speaking to the crowds that gathered at every station and meeting with local PPP officials on the train between stops. In spite of the doctor's orders to get plenty of rest, Bhutto spent up to 20 hours a day campaigning, trying to make up for the lack of sleep by taking medication and drinking large amounts of tea for her kidneys.

After returning to Karachi from the Punjab, Bhutto toured the rest of the country, campaigning not just for herself but for the other PPP candidates as well. Huge crowds attended her rallies. In Rawalpindi, more people went to hear her than had when she returned to Pakistan in 1986. Bhutto urged them to vote for the PPP: "You have to choose between reactionaries who want to suppress the people and the PPP which wants to break the chains of suppression." [104] But it was perhaps Begum Bhutto who had the best campaign line. She told supporters, "Ali Baba may be gone, but the forty thieves remain. . . . You know who they are. Vote the arrow [the PPP symbol] on November 16th." [105]

A WOMAN PRIME MINISTER

The fact that for 16 days the new president, Ghulam Ishaq Khan, was unable to form an anti-PPP coalition to head the government did not convince Bhutto's opponents that she should become prime minister. Not all of them objected to her on political grounds: Some felt that, at 35, she was too young to lead Pakistan, but some of her loudest critics objected to her because she was a woman. Before the elections, several religious leaders had issued fatwas, or judgments, telling people that it was against Islam for a woman to be the leader of a country. Even on the day of her inauguration, President Ishaq Khan did not hesitate to show his disdain for a woman: When Bhutto asked if she could join him for prayers at the mosque, he answered, "It's for men only," adding, "But you can watch."[106]

Bhutto was not sure how to respond to the attacks. "[T]he very mere fact that I was a woman seemed to drive them into a frenzy. So that was the biggest challenge. I don't know how to deal with that, I can deal with political differences, but how do you deal with it when someone says I don't like you because you're a woman and you've taken a man's place."[107] Nonetheless, Bhutto tried to defend herself. In a speech to the National Assembly, she reminded her opponents that Islamist parties had supported Fatima Jinnah (the sister of Pakistan's founder) for president in the 1965 elections. She also chose the title of *Mohtarma* for herself. Mohtarma means "esteemed lady" and implies that the lady is traditional and no longer young. Her best tactical move, however, was being received as prime minister by the king of Saudi Arabia only a month after she was sworn in. She gained legitimacy when "the ruler of the most Islamist of Islamic states and the Keeper of the Holy Shrines . . . formally received her as the head of the government of the Islamic Republic of Pakistan."[108]

Bhutto also made concessions to the Islamists that did not help win their approval. She became careful about her personal behavior, no longer shaking hands with men and asking other women in the administration to do the same. In public, she did not argue against the Islamists but spoke about the importance of Islam to Pakistan to show that she was qualified to lead an Islamic country. Some of her supporters thought that her efforts were pointless because she would never win the religious vote. For Bhutto, however, it was a way of avoiding unnecessary controversy.

When she took over as prime minister in December 1988, Bhutto's first priority was domestic policy and the first order of business was human rights. Political prisoners were set free, and those convicted of crimes by military courts had their cases reviewed. Although Bhutto did not have enough votes in the National Assembly to repeal Zia's constitutional amendments, his other laws were reviewed to make sure they were in accord with the constitution and respected human rights. Those that did not were repealed, and the special courts he had established were disbanded. Restrictions on labor unions were lifted, and student unions were allowed to reorganize. Free speech was also restored. Private news organizations were

FATIMA JINNAH

One of Pakistan's most beloved figures is Fatima Jinnah, the sister of the country's founder, Mohammed Ali Jinnah. She was born in 1893 and, despite family objections, received an excellent education with her brother's support. She attended the University of Calcutta, became a dentist, and opened a clinic in Bombay. When her brother was widowed in 1929, she went to live with him. They were close friends and companions for the rest of their lives.

Through her brother, Fatima Jinnah began to work for the All India Muslim League to gain independence from Britain. She was the principal founder of the All India Muslim Women Students Federation, which worked for the creation of Pakistan. In 1947, she founded the Women's Relief Committee to help refugees get established in their new country. Fatima Jinnah ran for president in 1965 against General Mohammed Ayub Khan. Although she lost the election, she had much popular support, and many believe that she would have won had the voting been conducted as one person—one vote instead of indirect election by members of local governing councils. Her fellow citizens gave her the title *Madar-i-Millat*, meaning "mother of the nation." She died in July 1967.

allowed to express their views, even if they were critical of the government. The government-owned media, however, continued to produce stories in support of the administration.

The Bhutto administration also addressed poverty. It built small, low-cost houses in big cities and opened health clinics. It also increased the education budget, building new schools around the country and hiring new teachers. School became compulsory, or mandatory, through the eighth grade. Bhutto also fought drug lords and the violence that goes with the drug trade. Her administration extended electrical service to thousands of rural villages. Although the PPP was still calling for social programs for the poor, Benazir Bhutto's economic policies were very different from her father's. Instead of nationalizing large companies, she tried to encourage small business start-ups and private investment in large industries.

Bhutto considered the work she did to improve the lives of Pakistani women her most important contributions. "[A]bove all I want to be remembered for what I did for women." [109] Her administration started family-planning programs. It opened police stations for women, recruiting women to serve as police officers, and set up a women's bank, run by women, that would provide loans to women who wanted to start their own businesses. It also required that 5 percent of employees in government offices be women.

In foreign affairs, Bhutto was not completely free to follow her own policies because she had to consult the army and the president on important issues. Bhutto and the others actually agreed on several issues, such as maintaining a strong alliance with the United States. Her first important task in foreign relations was hosting a summit meeting of the South Asian Association for Regional Cooperation (SAARC) in late December 1988, just a few weeks after she was sworn in. Bhutto was elected chair of the association.

The SAARC summit gave Bhutto and Indian Prime Minister Rajiv Gandhi an unusual opportunity to speak face to face.

The two young leaders got along well and were both eager to normalize relations between their countries. Unfortunately, in 1989, border disputes flared up again, as did violence in Kashmir. India and the United States were convinced that Pakistani army intelligence was sending aid to the Kashmiri rebels. This was entirely possible even though Bhutto had not ordered the army to do so. Her position was that the Kashmiris, who are mostly Muslim, should be allowed to vote in an internationally monitored plebiscite (a special vote undertaken by the whole country on a particular proposal, especially a government or ruler) to decide whether to be independent, part of Pakistan, or part of India. In the end, the disagreements could not be resolved and the mutual mistrust could not be overcome. All Bhutto and Gandhi were able to do was sign an agreement that neither side would attack the other's nuclear bases.

Afghanistan presented another serious problem for Pakistan in 1989. Pakistan wanted a stable and friendly government established in Afghanistan after the Soviet withdrawal. It also wanted to stem the flow of Afghan drugs through Pakistan, avoid the expense and disruption that would result if more Afghans came to Pakistan as refugees, and settle its border disputes with Afghanistan. Bhutto wanted to help establish a coalition government that would be acceptable to all the different groups in Afghanistan. All the parties did not have the same aims, however. For more than a year, Bhutto tried to get the different Afghan groups to negotiate a settlement, but they could not agree on how to share power. By 1990, religious fundamentalists who were later known as the Taliban were beginning to get the upper hand.

In other areas of foreign policy, Bhutto was more successful. She maintained good relations with China and reached an agreement by which China would build a nuclear power plant in Pakistan. China also agreed to transfer the technology so that Pakistan would be able to build its own plants in the future. Relations with the United Kingdom also improved, and

Pakistan rejoined the British Commonwealth. Bhutto traveled to England, where Prime Minister Margaret Thatcher welcomed Pakistan's return to democracy. Bhutto struck up a friendship with Thatcher that would last for years.

Relations with the United States proved to be more difficult. In June 1989, Bhutto went to Washington, D.C., on a state visit. President George H. W. Bush met with her, and she was invited to speak before a joint session of Congress (to both the House and Senate). She not only received a standing ovation, but also was assured of increased American aid to Pakistan—more than under Zia. After the Soviets left Afghanistan and Pakistan lost its strategic importance, however, Pakistan's nuclear program became a more important issue. Bhutto was unable to convince the United States that Pakistan was not building a nuclear weapon. The CIA director told her that the United States knew that Pakistan had already succeeded in building one. Soon after Bhutto's government was dissolved in August 1990, American aid was cut off.

As prime minister, Bhutto worked as tirelessly as ever, and her personal life continued to take second place to politics. In August 1989, she visited soldiers posted in the Siachen glacier, 20,000 feet high in the Himalayas, even though she was pregnant with her daughter, Bakhtwar. Bakhtwar was born in February 1990 during a new crisis over Kashmir. For once, the prime minister was forced to miss a meeting with opposition leaders in the NA to discuss the situation. Begum Bhutto took her place. Knowing full well that Bhutto was in the hospital recuperating, some opponents still complained that she had failed to attend.

BHUTTO'S GOVERNMENT UNRAVELS

Bhutto's term as prime minister ended as it had begun—in the midst of political battles and intrigue. The coalition she had forged with the Mohajir Quami Movement to form her government broke up when the PPP failed to carry out its promises to the other party. As a result, Bhutto lost her majority in the National Assembly and was unable to pass any legislation. She tried to govern by issuing ordinances, but President Ishaq Khan refused to sign them. The prime minister and the president clashed over various other issues as well, and Bhutto did not get along with the chief minister of the Punjab, Mohammed Nawaz Sharif, who refused to cooperate with the central government.

Bhutto also had problems with the army. Although she had regular briefings from the top leaders, she was kept away from the corps commanders and other officers, so she never established a relationship with many decision makers. She was not always included in important decisions, for example, General Aslam Beg and the president made the decision to build a nuclear bomb without consulting her. Bhutto's control of the army was minimal: "[I]f I came to know of something, I could restrain them and pull them in, but I was unable to promote or demote or punish any officer that was destabilising my government, leave alone violating government policy." [110]

Not all of the country's problems were political. Pakistan went into an economic decline during Bhutto's term, but the loan agreements the nation had with the International Monetary Fund (IMF) made it difficult to modify its economic policies. In addition, the oil boom in the Persian Gulf countries had ended, and Pakistanis could no longer go there for high-paying jobs that allowed them to send money home. Business was bad, and there were fewer jobs available.

Bhutto's administration made mistakes that put her at odds with the president, the army, and the government employees with whom she had to work. In her first press conference as prime minister, Bhutto promised to do away with the Eighth Amendment to the constitution, which gave the president his extensive powers. She failed to reorganize the army intelligence agencies and bring them under some civilian control when she had the chance. She appointed inexperienced advisors and staff whom she considered loyal but who often treated civil servants who had worked under Zia as if they were the enemy, and her government accepted political corruption as part of the system as ministers bent the rules to help friends and allies.

General Aslam Beg and his corps commanders made the decision to dismiss Benazir Bhutto. On August 6, 1990, the army took over Islamabad, and President Ghulam Ishaq Khan went on television to read the charges against her. He accused her of corruption, incompetence, and inappropriate conduct. He also dissolved the National Assembly, appointed a caretaker prime minister, and called for elections in October.

In October, the PPP lost control of the National Assembly, but Bhutto retained her seat. For the next three years, she was leader of the opposition to Prime Minister Nawaz Sharif. Soon, however, Nawaz Sharif clashed with Ishaq Khan over army appointments and tried to get the Eighth Amendment repealed. Ironically, both men tried to get the support of the PPP in their struggle. The president dropped all charges against Bhutto, and her husband, who had been jailed on various charges, was set free.

Bhutto, who was in London for the birth of her third child, consulted Margaret Thatcher about how to handle her enemies' offers. Thatcher advised, "Side with neither of them. . . . They will use you and dump you. Let them fight it out and bleed each other."[111] Bhutto listened but made up her own mind.

In April 1993, President Ishaq Khan once again dismissed a prime minister and his government. Nawaz Sharif took his case to the Supreme Court, which, in May, declared that the president did not have the right to dismiss him. The fight for power continued until the army finally intervened and worked out an agreement among the civilians that was approved by the PPP and the IJI (Islami Jamoori Ittehad or Islamic Democratic Alliance). Both Ishaq Khan and Nawaz Sharif were forced to step down, a caretaker prime minister was installed in July, and elections were scheduled for October 1993.

7

A Second Chance
1993–1997

How do we tackle population growth in a country like Pakistan?
We tackle it by tackling infant mortality. By providing villages
with electrification. By raising an army of women . . . to
educate our mothers, sisters, daughters in child welfare and
population control.

—Benazir Bhutto [112]

While Mohammed Nawaz Sharif and Ghulam Ishaq Khan bled
each other, Benazir Bhutto was already beginning her next
campaign. Bhutto had claimed all along that the 1990 elections
had been rigged and had been calling for new elections since.
By May 1993, she had signaled to Ishaq Khan that she would
support his reelection as president if he first supported hers as
prime minister—a move that upset many of her followers and
aides. Bhutto, however, was determined to put the government

back in the hands of the Pakistan People's Party with herself at the head.

Although some feared that she had lost her connection with the people after the disastrous defeat of the PPP in the previous elections, huge crowds continued to attend her rallies. Bhutto responded to them and they to her. An observer who accompanied her to a rally in Rawalpindi recalled how on the way there, Bhutto's car was mobbed by supporters throwing rose petals and other flowers at her and firing automatic weapons into the air:

> Tens of thousands of people filled the park, and others spilled into the surrounding streets and lanes; still others crowded on rooftops, and some hung from nearby trees. She waved and grinned as the crowds roared their approval—cheering, clapping, and stomping their feet. The din became deafening: more automatic weapons fired into the air, more fireworks filled the sky.[113]

Bhutto had not lost their love.

FAILURES AND TRIUMPHS

In October, the PPP once again became the ruling party by winning 86 seats in the National Assembly. Benazir Bhutto became the prime minister, although she did not have the two-thirds majority she needed to get rid of the Eighth Amendment. Nawaz Sharif was now the leader of a strong opposition. His party, the Pakistan Muslim League (PML/N), had 73 seats. Several smaller parties filled the remaining 58 seats. After she was sworn in, Bhutto did not support Ishaq Khan's reelection for president and he was forced into retirement. Instead, she put forward an old PPP loyalist, Farooq Ahmad Khan Leghari, who defeated the Muslim League candidate. With a president from her own party who claimed to be against the Eighth Amendment, Bhutto anticipated being able to finish her five-year term in office.

Another appointee whom she expected to be loyal was the new chief justice of the Supreme Court, Sajjad Ali Shah. Pakistan had a highly politicized judiciary, and it was assumed that he would rule in her favor. Disagreements with Shah, however, would cost Bhutto in the future.

In her second term, Bhutto found herself playing many of the same political games that she had played in her first term. Once again, she became embroiled in maintaining

THE EIGHTH AMENDMENT

The Eighth Amendment, passed in 1985, was designed to give Zia ul-Haq, as president, control of the government. The president, rather than the prime minister, was given the right to nominate provincial governors and judges to the Supreme Court and appellate courts, and in fact, he could nominate the prime minister. Although he did not take part in the day-to-day administration of government, he had to be kept informed about bills being considered and how the government was being run. The president also gained the right to issue ordinances, ask the prime minister to get a vote of confidence to show that he or she still had the support of the National Assembly, and set the date for elections. One of his most important powers was the right to appoint the heads of the different military services. Many of Zia's controversial Islamist laws calling for extreme punishments were contained in the Eighth Amendment. One of the most far-reaching clauses was the one that gave the president the power to dismiss the prime minister and the National Assembly. When Nawaz Sharif became prime minister in 1997, he quickly used his parliamentary majority to pass the Thirteenth Amendment, taking away the president's rights over the prime minister or the National Assembly. He did not change the parts that affected ordinary citizens.

control of the National Assembly and trying to get control of the three provincial assemblies the PPP did not head. Some deals, such as negotiating with religious leaders and parties to forestall problems because she was a woman, worked in her favor.

In early 1994, however, the PPP tried to get control of the Northwest Frontier Province by bribing several independent members of the legislature with ministries and other benefits if they joined the PPP in a coalition. The following year, the PPP tried to cut deals in Punjab to gain control of that assembly. Neither move worked, but both served to stain the party's—and Bhutto's—reputation. Her reputation was further damaged by the way her administration used the courts to harass political opponents with charges of corruption—a strategy she had condemned during Nawaz Sharif's tenure. She was plagued by demonstrations and strikes that Nawaz Sharif staged to protest her government.

One of the most serious problems her administration faced was street violence. Ethnic tensions had existed in Sindh for a long time, and the Mohajir Quami Movement (MQM) had been formed to protect the rights of the *mohajirs,* or immigrants from India and their descendants, but the MQM had never been able to reach a workable arrangement for more power with either Bhutto or Nawaz Sharif. The tensions escalated dramatically when the MQM split into two factions that began to battle each other in the streets of Karachi and other cities. Under Nawaz Sharif, the army had not been able to put a stop to the violence, and, by 1994, business had almost come to a stop in Karachi. The Bhutto administration finally sent in special forces, who worked with police to crush the MQM. The fights between factions stopped, but government forces were accused of using extreme violence—about 1,800 people were reportedly killed—and the underlying tensions never disappeared completely.

Pakistan continued to face grave economic problems. It had a tremendous budget deficit—the government spent much more money than it took in—and the IMF was unwilling to release loans unless the government took major steps to reduce it. Bhutto tried to get the money by establishing a general sales tax that would be charged on most items. The tax was unpopular with both producers and consumers and could not get through the legislature. Many poor, working, and business people resented the fact that the agricultural income of feudal landlords would not be taxed. Nevertheless, Bhutto was able reduce the deficit and reached an agreement with the IMF, but the deficit combined with inflation (a continuing rise in prices) to create more economic problems

Relations with the United States, however, improved considerably during President Bill Clinton's first term and Bhutto's second, and that brought some economic relief. American companies invested several billion dollars in Pakistan, particularly in energy production. The two countries also began cooperating on the problems of illegal drugs and international terrorism. Pakistan extradited several wanted criminals, including Ramzi Yousef, the man responsible for the 1993 bombing of the World Trade Center in New York.

Modernizing the country and improving social services were major policies of Bhutto's second administration. Private companies were brought into the energy industry, and the first privately owned power plant was built. Electricity was extended to almost every village in the country, and new gas pipelines were laid in many areas. The World Bank called Bhutto's energy initiatives a model for the rest of the developing world. Seven hundred thousand new telephone numbers were added, and FM radio, cellular phones, and satellite dishes were used for the first time.

Women and children once again benefited from the Bhutto administration. Schools were a priority: 21,000 primary and

3,000 secondary schools were built. Several women were appointed as judges to superior courts, and more computer centers were opened for women. Some of Bhutto's most far-reaching programs were in the area of health. Through her Polio Vaccination Program, almost all children under the age of five were immunized, and she restored the country's Tuberculosis Control Program. One of her most innovative plans trained Lady Health Visitors to teach other women—particularly in the country—about childcare and family planning in order to reduce infant mortality and improve maternal health. Bhutto also wanted to reduce the high birth rate, which the country could not afford. She explained,

> We brought down the population growth rate by one-third, and because of the cascading effect it's going to continue going downwards. And there was a lot of hue and cry against the population program, but we did it by recruiting 50,000 women from different villages. . . . [W]e had ambassadors everywhere to counter people in villages who were opposed to population control.[114]

Bhutto received the World Health Organization's highest honor, the Health-for-All Gold Medal for her work in public health.

FAMILY TROUBLES

After Bhutto was elected prime minister, her brother Mir Murtaza returned to Pakistan and won a seat in the Sindh Provincial Assembly. After publicly supporting her son as a leader in Sindh—Benazir's power base—Nusrat Bhutto lost her position as cochair of the PPP and Benazir became sole leader. Benazir and Mir Murtaza had never agreed on many political issues, but during her second term, the disagreements reached the point that he publicly accused her and her husband of corruption. Mir Murtaza blamed Zardari for the financial crookedness in her government, and it became public knowledge that the two men hated each other. On September 20, 1996, Mir Murtaza's motorcade was stopped by a large contingent of police near 70 Clifton. A shootout between his guards and the police ensued. Six of his guards were killed, and Mir Murtaza was wounded. After 40 minutes, he was finally taken to a hospital—one not equipped to handle a case like his—where he died soon after. The police disposed of all the evidence before it could be examined.

Bhutto's supporters and opponents agreed that the prime minister's brother could not have been murdered without the approval of someone highly placed in the government. The question was, who? Many of Murtaza's supporters blamed Bhutto, to whom he presented a serious challenge within the PPP as an equally legitimate heir of Zulfikar Ali Bhutto—perhaps more so because he was a son. Bhutto herself blamed the president; Leghari had been questioning the policies of the Bhutto administration for some time in private and by 1996 had publicly distanced himself from the prime minister. Some of her supporters blamed her opponents, who now had only one Bhutto to deal with. They believed her life was in danger.

Six weeks later, in November 1996, President Leghari used the Eighth Amendment to dismiss Benazir Bhutto's government. The charges included corruption, abuse of power, and harassment of the opposition. She was also accused of ridiculing the Supreme Court, using extreme violence during the MQM crackdown, and never prosecuting the guilty officers. Leghari accused Bhutto of not respecting his authority. That night, 20 people were arrested for taking part in Mir Murtaza's murder. Among them were high-ranking members of the PPP, the chief of police of Karachi, and Asif Zardari, who was accused of ordering the murder.

The PPP regained control of the National Assembly in 1993, and Bhutto (shown here speaking in 1995) became prime minister once again. But this government fared little better than her first: her brother's death in 1996 aroused suspicion, even among her supporters, and less than two months later her government was dissolved for the second time. The scandal surrounding her brother's death eroded her power in the National Assembly, and charges of corruption have troubled Bhutto and her husband ever since.

The Supreme Court, under Chief Justice Shah, declined Bhutto's petition to have her government reinstated. New elections, in which Nawaz Sharif and the Pakistan Muslim

League trounced the PPP, were held in February 1997. Bhutto claimed that the election was rigged but went back to the National Assembly to lead the opposition.

She did so under the shadow of very damaging corruption charges. Dismissed governments in Pakistan were always charged with corruption, but this time not even her friends denied the charges. Particularly damaging was the charge of financial corruption, which not only Mir Murtaza but also Nusrat Bhutto had privately warned about earlier. Bhutto and Zardari were accused of having received millions of dollars in kickbacks (the return of part of the money received for a contract) from businesses that received government contracts. Zardari had developed a bad reputation: He was known as Mr. 10 Percent during Bhutto's first administration and Mr. 20 Percent during her second for the amount he expected back from each contract. In June 1996, the financial corruption became a public scandal when a British newspaper printed a series of stories claiming that Zardari had set up a foreign bank account and bought a number of expensive apartments and a mansion abroad. Bhutto and Zardari denied making the purchases. After Bhutto's dismissal, the new government began investigating the allegations of corruption and charged them in various different cases.

Bhutto lost many of her loyal supporters. Many people who, like her, had been through jail and exile and sacrificed their family life were disenchanted with her. Some felt that, by getting mired in patronage and battles for control, she had betrayed the ideals and principles they had all labored for. Some felt that she was not capable of solving the country's long-term economic and ethnic problems. Others felt that she had given up her democratic principles and become autocratic. A year after her dismissal, one analyst explained, "[Her supporters] feel that Benazir has turned the party into a one-woman show, where allegiance to Ms. Bhutto is more important than the wishes of the large and dedicated party membership."[115] Bhutto herself admitted that she may have pushed too hard:

> I . . . tried to be very aggressive and warmongering [with my people] in my second term to try and co-opt my opposition. I am a consensus sort of person, I like to win people over. Not to compromise the core of my values, but I seek the middle way and I tried to do that. I think in retrospect it was wrong because I did not co-opt them and I alienated some of my own supporters. But at the same time we got the three years to eliminate polio, to build schools and electrify villages.[116]

Many of her friends, however, were appalled by the apparent financial dealings of Asif Zardari.

8

The Work Continues

1997–Present

[I]t is difficult to visualize Pakistan politics, for the next few years at least, without Benazir, whether she is in or out of government.

—Iqbal Akhund [117]

After becoming prime minister in February 1997, Nawaz Sharif acted quickly to expand his power. In April, the Thirteenth Amendment, taking away presidential powers, was passed. In May, the power to investigate corruption charges against members of government was taken from an independent commission and placed in the hands of the National Accountability Bureau, which worked under Nawaz Sharif. In August, the Anti-Terrorism Act, which enabled the police or army to make searches and arrests without warrants, was passed.

For a little over two years, Benazir Bhutto led the opposition in the National Assembly. She spoke aggressively and critically of the government and its policies even though she was heckled by the great majority of members. In a diary, she described a speech she gave during the budget debates for 1997:

> I mention that the politics of revenge has frightened capital and paralyzed the economy. I begin to give a few examples. When I mention my political secretary, who has been imprisoned and freed on court orders three times, off-loaded from a flight once, tortured and asked to lie about me, the . . . [ruling party] benches burst into an uproar.
>
> I shout as loud as I can over the microphone, "Sir [Mr. Speaker], why do they panic every time they hear the name of a woman?" That shuts them up. At least temporarily. [118]

Her opponents also had their turn to criticize her and her views and were able to harass her and her political allies. One such small annoyance was that the Speaker did not allow her budget speech to be shown on television. Another was that the electricity of her Islamabad house, where she had her office, was regularly cut off at odd times, preventing her and her staff from running fans or using their computers. Far worse were the jailings and kidnappings. When Bhutto gave her budget speech, her husband had been in jail for eight months without having been indicted for any crime. One of the opposition leaders of the Sindh provincial assembly had been kidnapped the week before and not been found.

Bhutto continued to work long hours. She shuttled back and forth between Karachi, where the children were, and Islamabad, where the government met. She would write speeches on airplanes and consult other PPP leaders by phone. Relaxation was a few minutes playing with her cats or a late night cup of tea with a friend, even if the conversation did not stray too far from politics.

Her children were also a serious worry for Bhutto, because her constant traveling did not just affect her. As she was leaving once for the capital, she was shocked to hear seven-year-old

Bakhtwar breezily say, "Bye, it was nice seeing you. Come back soon," as if Bhutto were a mere acquaintance.[119] Hearing her child distance herself emotionally pained Bhutto. It also pained her when four-year-old Aseefa told her, "Mama, I cry every night when you are away and Baba [Papa] is in jail."[120] In those days, only Bilawal seemed secure. Although she could reassure the girls that she loved them, even a strong political fighter like Bhutto could not always deflect the unintended arrows of her own children. When the children heard that she would be 44 on her next birthday, Bakhtwar commented, "That's as old as a dinosaur." All the exhausted mother could think was, "I don't have the strength to reply."[121]

Bhutto also feared for her children's safety. She thought that the economic problems of the country might lead people to demonstrate and even storm the houses of politicians. That fall, Bhutto put the children in school in Dubai, in the United Arab Emirates, which was only an hour and a half from Karachi by plane—close enough for her to visit them. Her life was now divided among three cities: Dubai, Islamabad, and Karachi, where Zardari was jailed. Zardari did win a symbolic legal battle against the administration: He had been elected senator the previous March, while still in prison, and in December 1997, Nawaz Sharif was forced to let him be sworn in, although Zardari still was not released. Bhutto continued fighting the accusations against her and serving in the National Assembly for more than a year. In April 1999, however, she and Zardari were convicted of corruption in a case involving a Swiss company called SGS/Cotecna and sentenced to five years in prison. To avoid being jailed, she joined the children in Dubai that same month.

RETURN OF MILITARY RULE

Nawaz Sharif was removed from power on October 12, 1999, when he tried to oust the chief of army staff, General Pervez Musharraf. The general imprisoned Nawaz Sharif and sent him into exile in December 2000. Musharraf declared himself president in 2001. Then, in April 2002, he held a referendum in which voting "yes" would give him five more years as president. Because there was no other candidate, he won.

Once Musharraf took power, Bhutto—from exile—began hammering at the need to restore democracy. A freely elected democratic government, she said, was the only way to prevent religious extremists from becoming the only alternative to a military dictator. She cited Iran under the ayatollahs and Afghanistan under the Taliban as examples of how easily this could happen.

President Musharraf called for parliamentary elections in October 2002. Prior to the elections, however, he enacted laws that disqualified both Bhutto and Nawaz Sharif from running again. He also added 29 new amendments to the constitution, including changes that gave him a five-year term extension and the power to dissolve the parliament. They also gave the army a formal role in government. As the elections approached, the PPP once again emerged as the most popular party in Pakistan. Bhutto hoped to run in spite of the president's threat to have her jailed if she returned. Her lawyers challenged the laws preventing her return, but the court ruled against her.

Shortly before the elections, Bhutto was voted chair of the Pakistan People's Party for life. After the election, the party once again sat in opposition but without Bhutto to lead it. New policies and strategies therefore had to be devised through international consultation, and Bhutto has managed to hold the party together from abroad. She continues to be actively involved in parliamentary affairs, giving specific directions on how the party should proceed. She regularly writes position papers for the party on domestic and foreign policy, and she tends to be very critical of General Musharraf. She is also deeply involved in the day-to-day running of the PPP.

Bhutto continues to be an international figure in her own right. She is once again regarded as Pakistan's most popular politician and the only one with supporters in all four provinces. She still has friends in high places, such as President Olusegun Obasanjo of Nigeria, who invited her to be keynote speaker at a

Although the allegations of corruption that forced her into exile in the late 1990s have not yet been resolved, Bhutto remains politically active. As permanent leader of the PPP, she guides the party's strategy. She also works to expand and protect women's rights in the Islamic world. Loyal Bhutto supporters continue to call for her return to power; this group, from the Women's Wing of the PPP, protested her conviction in the Swiss courts in 2003.

national celebration in March 2003. She travels to many countries, giving interviews and speeches. Since the late 1990s, Bhutto has been explaining to Western audiences how Muslims perceive the United States and Europe and the dangers that religious extremists present. She has called the growth of religious and ethnic violence the most serious problem of the twenty-first century.

Bhutto continues to press the issue of women's rights in Muslim countries and elsewhere. She speaks out against the crushing discrimination that women often face in the developing world. In her speeches, she encourages young women to believe that they can achieve as much as any man. Reflecting on her own youth, she has noted how the world is changing, "[N]ow 30 years down the line, I think we can be more comfortable with the notion that it is no longer only a man's world. There are quite a few women out there and we women can start being more like women, we don't have to outdistance or outperform men, we can start being confident about ourselves."[122] For Bhutto, the key to women's success is education: "If women are truly to be defined by themselves and their own accomplishments and abilities, they need the level of education that empowers them. Education leads to the kind of financial independence that causes women to break the shackles of being only a man's daughter or a man's wife."[123]

THE CORRUPTION QUESTION

The charges of corruption have followed her through the years. The two-year investigation conducted by the Nawaz Sharif administration produced a great deal of bad publicity for Bhutto and Zardari. Although some of the accusations were absurd, the Accountability Board appeared to have documents proving that the couple had received more than $1.5 billion in kickbacks.

WOMEN IN PAKISTAN

The civil and political rights that women have in the Muslim world vary widely from country to country. In Pakistan, the constitution guarantees women rights equal to men's. Tradition, however, dictates that women should obey their fathers and husbands. Women in wealthy and educated families generally command more respect and have more freedom than poor women. Many upper- and middle-class women have careers, and status and education can affect even the way they dress: Women in the upper ranks do not always cover their heads or even wear a *dupatta,* or head scarf, outdoors, but poor women tend to wear burkas in public. Even among the upper classes, however, religious laws are sometimes used to control women's behavior. In one famous case, a father tried to dissolve his adult daughter's marriage to a man whom he had not approved.

After their conviction by the Lahore High Court in the SGS/ Cotecna case in 1999, Bhutto and Zardari appealed to the Supreme Court. It dismissed the conviction in April 2001, when transcripts of several audiotapes showing that one of the judges in the original trial had negotiated with the senior investigator in the Accountability Bureau over Bhutto and Zardari's punishment before they had even been found guilty were printed in a British newspaper. Musharraf asked for a retrial of the SGS/Cotecna case and for speeded up trials in nine other corruption cases. When she failed to return to Pakistan to appear in court in the new trials, Bhutto was sentenced to three years in prison.

Asif Zardari has never been released from jail. He has been tortured or denied medical assistance at different times. Since 1996, he has been accused in 19 different criminal cases, including drugs, murder, corruption, and tax evasion. Each time he becomes eligible for bail, new charges are brought against him. Despite his reputation, Zardari has been convicted in only one kickback case, which was under appeal in the fall of 2003. Bhutto has admitted that her husband may have behaved improperly but insists that his actions were not criminal.

The legal battles have taken a heavy toll on Bhutto's family. The children have not seen their father for years, although they do exchange letters and cards. Zardari is allowed one hour per week on the phone with his wife, half an hour with his three children. Their conversations are tapped. Bhutto has been offered his freedom if she gives up politics. Her answer is still "no," the same as when she was the prisoner.

LOOKING BACK

Reflecting on her past political life, Bhutto sees better ways in which she could have handled problems. She has conceded,

> I didn't get on with the president [during my first term] because he wanted to have a kind of presidential system and I believed in the parliamentary system. Then I

remember a later president who was from my own party. I think of the amount of power I gave him, and he treated me so shabbily. If I had given the first president half the powers that I gave my own president, maybe he would not have knocked us out, and democracy could have taken stronger root.[124]

She also regrets not having done something about government corruption.

For Bhutto, however, politics is not about obtaining wealth or power:

> [P]olitics is an obsession. You cannot just be in politics . . . it is not an eight to five job. It's an around the clock job. So if it was just power I think it would be very empty. I think idealism is very important. The need to change, to bring about change. . . . I think it is very, very important to have ideals, because when one has ideals one thinks the suffering is worth it.[125]

She warns, though, that in politics, one cannot always expect to get everything one works for. Other people do not always agree about what is best, so it becomes necessary to compromise.

Bhutto also points out that the compromises are not only political:

> When I was growing up I thought a woman could have it all and now I find that yes a woman can have it all but she has to be prepared to pay the price. And the price means a lot of guilt about not being there for your children when they need you, a lot of tension also with your husband on work schedules. So you find you can have a husband, you can have a family, you can have a career but . . . you have very little time left for yourself.[126]

Bhutto does not want her children to go into politics, although she admits it is difficult to get her point across. "I want to protect them from the tragedies that I have seen in my life, but they are growing up in a political home. They see politicians all the time."[127] She would much prefer for them to go to college and then study a profession, to follow a different path. "The world is changing, and I think that in the new global century you can have a career [in public service] without being in government. Through NGOs [nongovernmental organizations] and community service there's a great deal that can be done."[128]

Having children also changes some of the choices she can make for herself. She cannot take the kinds of risks she took in the days of General Zia. Her own safety has become important for the children's sake. With their father in jail, she had powerful personal reasons to go into exile in 1999: One parent had to be free to look after the children.

What sustains her through the worry and the years of separation is her faith in God. The manner in which extremists use Islam to subjugate women troubles her deeply because "Islam forbids injustice; injustice against people, against nations, against women."[129] In trying to break her will, Zia's Islamist regime helped her find strength through faith. When she was denied all material things in prison, she "realized that they can't take God away from me. . . . [F]rom that moment I realized that God is always with one, so what gave me the faith and sustenance was my belief that God places a burden on people to bear and He places only that burden which they *can* bear."[130] Bhutto has borne her burden through the years in spite of its size and scope. "I'm not saying that there have not been moments of great [personal] triumph and great happiness. . . . But there have been far more moments when I have found myself embroiled in a life larger than my own, on a much larger canvas. In a sense, my life has not been my own."[131] Part of that larger canvas is the people who throw rose petals at her and throng to meet her. They help to sustain her, to lighten the burden. "Maybe I'm a needy person, maybe I need love. . . . When I get so much love at the mass level, I feel that I must go on."[132]

Bhutto has advised those who wish to be leaders to be prepared to carry burdens and point the way. "Leaders *lead*, remember that," she says. "Convince, educate, bring people around to do what is moral, to do what is right, to do what is necessary." She added, "[D]on't be afraid to stand out and stand up."[133] Leaders must also pay attention to their supporters. "[I]n the past when I used to meet people I used to want to tell them what we were doing. Now I realize that you have to listen to people and what they are saying we ought to be doing, because that's the feedback."[134]

A leader also needs emotional resources to keep going in spite of obstacles and disappointments. Bhutto stated, "I think leadership is very much predicated on the capacity to absorb defeat and overcome it. Now, after having been in politics for more than two decades, I have come to the strong conclusion that the difference between somebody who succeeds and somebody who fails is the ability to absorb a setback."[135] Defeats and setbacks will inevitably occur. When they do, a leader must be willing to face them and analyze what went wrong. "Each time one is in trouble or hits rock bottom, it's a time for reflection. I think being able to climb back depends very much on the ability to reflect and see how the world has changed, because it's going to go on changing."[136]

Benazir Bhutto has faced many defeats in her life. She has made serious mistakes, and she has done good things for her country. Even though her personal integrity has been questioned, she has not retreated. She has faced the questions with courage—the way she faced prison and the attacks of political opponents. Benazir Bhutto has absorbed many setbacks, but she perseveres.

Chronology

1953 Benazir Bhutto is born on June 21 to Nusrat Isphahani Bhutto and Zulfikar Ali Bhutto.

1971 Zulfikar Ali Bhutto becomes president of Pakistan.

1972 Benazir Bhutto attends the Simla Summit with her father.

1973 The Pakistani constitution is adopted.

1973 Zulfikar Ali Bhutto becomes prime minister of Pakistan.

1973 Benazir Bhutto graduates from Radcliffe College, Harvard University.

1977 Bhutto graduates from Oxford University.

1979 Zulfikar Ali Bhutto is executed by military dictator Mohammed Zia ul-Haq.

1979–1980 Benazir and Nusrat Bhutto are placed under house arrest.

1981 Bhutto is put in solitary confinement in prison under primitive conditions.

1982–1984 Bhutto is placed in solitary confinement under house arrest.

1984 Bhutto is exiled to Europe; she takes over Pakistan People's Party.

1986 Bhutto triumphantly returns to Pakistan.

1987 Benazir Bhutto marries Asif Ali Zardari.

1988 Bhutto is elected prime minister for the first time.

1990 Benazir Bhutto's government is dissolved by President Ghulam Ishaq Khan.

1993 Bhutto is elected prime minister for the second time.

1996 Bhutto's government is dissolved by President Farooq Leghari.

1999 Bhutto goes into self-imposed exile.

2002 Bhutto becomes lifetime chairperson of the Pakistan People's Party.

Notes

CHAPTER 1

1. Peter W. Galbraith, "The Return of Benazir Bhutto," *Harvard Magazine,* July–August 1989, p. 20.

2. Josee Dupuis, "Benazir Bhutto," *Women of Influence,* July 2002, *http://www.cbc.ca/national/news/ womenof influence/bhutto.html.*

3. Women in Power Reveal What It Takes, Pregnancy and Politics. *http://www.bbc.co.uk/worldservice/ people/features/wiwp/dyncon/ bhutto.shtml.*

4. Muhammed Ali Shaikh, *Benazir Bhutto: A Political Biography.* Karachi, Pakistan: Orient Books Publishing House, 2000, p. 123.

5. Ibid., p. 124.

6. Mary Anne Weaver, *Pakistan: In the Shadow of Jihad and Afghanistan.* New York: Farrar, Straus, and Giroux, 2002, p. 193.

7. Iqbal Akhund, *Trial and Error: The Advent and Eclipse of Benazir Bhutto.* Oxford: Oxford University Press, 2000, p. 318.

8. Ibid., p. 317.

CHAPTER 2

9. "Benazir Bhutto: Interview," *The Hall of Public Service.* October 27, 2000, http://www.achievement.org/ autodoc/page/bhu0int-1.

10. Benazir Bhutto, *Daughter of Destiny,* New York: Simon and Schuster, 1989, p. 38.

11. "Benazir Bhutto: Interview," *http://www.achievement.org/ autodoc/page/bhu0int-1.*

12. Shaikh, *Benazir Bhutto,* p. 25.

13. Bhutto, *Daughter,* p. 43.

14. Ibid., p. 44.

15. Ibid.

16. Shaikh, *Benazir Bhutto,* p. 28.

17. Bhutto, *Daughter,* p. 48.

18. Ibid.

19. "Benazir Bhutto: Interview," http://www.achievement.org/aut odoc/page/bhu0int-1.

20. Bhutto, *Daughter,* p. 45.

21. Shaikh, *Benazir Bhutto,* p. 29.

22. "Benazir Bhutto: Interview," http://www.achievement.org/aut odoc/page/bhu0int-1.

23. Bhutto, *Daughter,* p. 46.

24. Ibid., p. 50

25. "Benazir Bhutto: Interview," *http://www.achievement.org/ autodoc/page/bhu0int-1.*

26. Bhutto, *Daughter,* p. 51.

27. Ibid., 52.

28. Ibid., p. 53.

29. Ibid., p. 52.

30. "Benazir ('Pinkie') Bhutto." *Harvard Magazine.* July–August 1989, p. 3.

CHAPTER 3

31. Bhutto, *Daughter,* p. 59.

32. Ibid., p. 58.

33. Ibid., p. 60.

34. Ibid.

35. Shaikh, *Benazir Bhutto,* p. 41.

36. Ibid., p. 42.

37. Galbraith, "Return," p. 20.

38. Bhutto, *Daughter*, p. 59

39. Ibid.

40. Ibid., p. 61.

41. Ibid.

42. Galbraith, "Return," p. 20.

43. Bhutto, *Daughter*, p. 66.

44. Ibid., p. 67.

45. Galbraith, "Return," p. 20.

46. Ibid.

47. "Benazir Bhutto: Interview," *http://www.achievement.org/ autodoc/page/bhu0int-1*.

48. Ibid.

49. Bhutto, *Daughter*, p. 70.

50. Ibid., p. 71.

51. Ibid., p. 72.

52. Ibid.

53. Ibid., p. 76.

54. Ibid., p. 77.

55. Ibid.

56. Ibid., p. 80.

57. Ibid.

58. Shaikh, *Benazir Bhutto*, p. 69.

59. Bhutto, *Daughter*, p. 80.

60. Ibid., p. 85.

61. Ibid., p. 86.

62. Ibid., p. 83.

63. Ibid., p. 3.

64. Ibid., p. 93.

65. Ibid., p. 98.

CHAPTER 4

66. Ibid., p. 113.

67. Ibid., p. 90.

68. Anwar H. Syed, *The Discourse and Politics of Zulfikar Ali Bhutto*. New York: St. Martin's Press, p. 12.

69. Bhutto, *Daughter*, p. 102.

70. Ibid., p. 104.

71. Ibid.

72. Ibid., p. 115.

73. Ibid., p. 125.

74. Ibid., p. 131.

75. Ibid., p. 132.

76. Weaver, *Pakistan*, p. 178.

77. "Benazir Bhutto: Interview," *http://www.achievement.org/ autodoc/page/bhu0int-1*.

CHAPTER 5

78. Omar Noman, *Pakistan: A Political and Economic History since 1947*. London: Kegan Paul International, 1990, p. 120.

79. Chart on Noman, *Pakistan*, p. 123.

80. Akhund, *Trial and Error*, p. 321.

81. Weaver, *Pakistan*, p. 186.

82. Ibid.

83. Bhutto, *Daughter*, p. 200.

84. Ibid.

85. Ibid., p. 205.

86. Ibid., p. 202.

87. Ibid.

88. Ibid.

89. Ibid., p. 206.

90. Ibid., p. 213.

91. Ibid., p. 231.

92. Ibid., p. 244.

Notes

93. Galbraith, "Return," p. 24.

94. Bhutto, *Daughter,* p. 259.

95. Ibid., p. 277.

96. Ibid., p. 322.

97. Ibid., p. 324.

98. Ibid., p. 326.

99. Ibid., p. 359.

100. Ibid., p. 357.

CHAPTER 6

101. Ibid., p. 344.

102. Ibid., p. 379.

103. Ibid., p. 387.

104. Ibid. p. 392.

105. Ibid.

106. Weaver, *Pakistan,* p. 192.

107. "Benazir Bhutto, Former Prime Minister of Pakistan," *Women in Power Reveal What It Takes,* Dealing With Criticism and Conflict. *http://www.bbc.co.uk/worldservice/people/features/wiwp/dyncon/bhutto.shtml.*

108. Akhund, *Trial and Error,* p. 90.

109. "Benazir Bhutto, Former Prime Minister of Pakistan," *Women in Power Reveal What It Takes,* Policies for Women. *http://www.bbc.co.uk/worldservice/people/features/wiwp/dyncon/bhutto.shtml*

110. Tony Jones, "Benazir Bhutto speaks to Lateline about attack on Iraq." *Lateline* Australian Broadcasting Corporation, *http://www.abc.net.au/lateline/s609909.htm.*

111. Weaver, *Pakistan,* 185.

CHAPTER 7

112. United Nations Population Information Network, "94-09-07: Statement of Pakistan, H.E. Mohtarma Benazir Bhutto." *http://www.un.org/popin/icpd/conference/gov/940907211416.html.*

113. Weaver, *Pakistan,* 173.

114. "Benazir Bhutto: Interview," *http://www.achievement.org/autodoc/page/bhu0int-1.*

115. Hans Zomer, "It's Hard to Be an Opposition Leader: The Politics of Benazir Bhutto, Politician and Icon." One World News Service. *http://www.oneworld.org/owe/news/owns/hz2_en.htm.*

116. "Benazir Bhutto: Interview," *http://www.achievement.org/autodoc/page/bhu0int-1.*

CHAPTER 8

117. Akhund, *Trial and Error,* p. 325.

118. *Slate,* "Benazir Bhutto." *Diary: A Weeklong Electronic Journal,* June 17, 1997 to June 21, 1997. *http://slate.msn.com/id/3731/entry/24703.*

119. Ibid., *http://slate.msn.com/id/3731/entry/24702.*

120. Ibid., *http://slate.msn.com/id/3731/entry/24705.*

121. Ibid., *http://slate.msn.com/id/3731,* Saturday 10/21/97.

122. "Benazir Bhutto: Former Prime Minister of Pakistan," *Women in Power Reveal What It Takes. http://www.bbc.co.uk/worldservice/people/features/wiwp/dyncon/bhutto.shtml.*

123. Benazir Bhutto, "Victims of Terrorism." Speech delivered December 16, 2002 on U.S. Tour. *http://ppp.org.pk/speeches/speech48.*

124. "Benazir Bhutto: Interview," *http://www.achievement.org/autodoc/page/bhu0int-1.*

125. Ibid.

126. "Benazir Bhutto: Former Prime Minister of Pakistan," *http://www.bbc.co.uk/worldservice/people/features/wiwp/dyncon/bhutto.shtml.*

127. "Benazir Bhutto: Interview," *http://www.achievement.org/autodoc/page/bhu0int-1.*

128. Ibid.

129. Benazir Bhutto, "Labels, Discrimination and Intolerance as Betrayers of Islam," *Women at the Podium: Memorable Speeches in History,* ed. S. Michele Nix. New York: HarperCollins, 2000, p. 362.

130. "Benazir Bhutto: Interview," *http://www.achievement.org/autodoc/page/bhu0int-1.*

131. Weaver, *Pakistan,* p. 179.

132. "Benazir Bhutto: Interview," *http://www.achievement.org/autodoc/page/bhu0int-1.*

133. Bhutto, "Victims of Terrorism," *http://ppp.org.pk/speeches/speech48.*

134. "Benazir Bhutto: Interview," http://*www.achievement.org/autodoc/page/bhu0int-1.*

135. Ibid.

136. Ibid.

Bibliography

Books and Periodicals

Akhund, Iqbal. *Trial and Error: The Advent and Eclipse of Benazir Bhutto.* Oxford: Oxford University Press, 2000.

"Benazir ('Pinkie') Bhutto." *Harvard Magazine.* July–August 1989, p. 3.

Bhutto, Benazir. *Daughter of Destiny.* New York: Simon and Schuster, 1989.

———. "Labels Discrimination and Intolerance as Betrayers of Islam," in *Women at the Podium: Memorable Speeches in History,* ed. S. Michele Nix. New York: HarperCollins, 2000.

Galbraith, Peter W. "The Return of Benazir Bhutto." *Harvard Magazine.* July–August 1989, p. 19.

Jones, Owen Bennett. *Pakistan: Eye of the Storm.* New Haven: Yale University Press, 2002.

Noman, Omar. *Pakistan: A Political and Economic History Since 1947.* London: Kegan Paul International, 1990.

Shaikh, Muhammed Ali. *Benazir Bhutto: A Political Biography.* Karachi: Orient Books Publishing House, 2000.

Syed, Anwar H. *The Discourse and Politics of Zulfikar Ali Bhutto.* New York: St. Martin's Press, 1992.

Weaver, Mary Anne. *Pakistan: In the Shadow of Jihad and Afghanistan.* New York: Farrar, Straus and Giroux, 2002.

Websites

Academy of Achievement. "Benazir Bhutto: Interview." *The Hall of Public Service.* October 27, 2000. *http://www.achievement.org/autodoc/page/bhu0int-1.*

Bhutto, Benazir. "Victims of Terrorism." speech delivered December 16, 2002 on U.S. Tour. *http://www.ppp.org.pk/speeches/speech48.html.*

"Benazir Bhutto: Former Prime Minister of Pakistan." *Women in Power Reveal What It Takes. http://www.bbc.co.uk/worldservice/people/features/wiwp/dyncon/bhutto.shtml.*

Dupuis, Josee. "Benazir Bhutto." *Women of Influence,* July 2002. *http://www.cbc.ca/national/news/womenofinfluence/bhutto.html.*

Jones, Tony. "Benazir Bhutto speaks to Lateline about attack on Iraq." *Lateline.* Australian Broadcasting Corporation. Broadcast July 17, 2002. *http://www.abc.net.au/lateline/s609909.htm.*

McCarthy, Rory. "Dutiful Daughter of the East." August 28, 2002. *http://www.smh.com.au/articles/2002/08/27/1030053058789.html.*

Slate. "Benazir Bhutto." *Diary: A Weeklong Electronic Journal,* June 17, 1997, to June 21, 1997. *http://slate.msn.com/id/3731/entry/24702, http://slate.msn.com/id/3731/entry/24703, http://slate.msn.com/ id/3731/entry/24704, http://slate.msn.com/id/3731/entry/24705, http://slate.msn.com/id/3731/*

United Nations Population Information Network. "94-09-07: Statement of Pakistan, H.E. Mohtarma Benazir Bhutto." *http://www.un.org/ popin/icpd/conference/gov/940907211416.html.*

Further Reading

Afkhami, Mahnaz, and Erika Friedl, eds. *Muslim Women and the Politics of Participation: Implementing the Beijing Platform.* Syracuse, NY: Syracuse University Press, 1997.

Ali, M. M. "In Pakistan Benazir Bhutto's Dismissal is Deja Vu All Over Again." *Washington Report.* January/February 1997. *http://washington-report. org/backissues/0197/9701011.htm.*

Ghazali, Abdus Sattar. *Islamic Pakistan: Illusions & Reality.* Islamabad, Pakistan: National Book Club, 1999. *http://ghazali.net/book1/.*

Morris, Harvey. "The West and Islam: An Interview with Benazir Bhutto," *Foreign Wire.com. http://www.foreignwire.com/benazir.html.*

Visram, Rozina. *Women in India and Pakistan: The Struggle for Independence from British Rule.* Cambridge: Cambridge University Press, 1992.

World Health Organization. "Health-for-All Gold Medal Awarded to Prime Minister of Pakistan." *http://www.who.int/archives/inf-pr-1996/pr96-66. html.* [Press release]

Zomer, Hans. "It's Hard to Be an Opposition Leader: The Politics of Benazir Bhutto, Politician and Icon." One World News Service. *http://www.oneworld.org/owe/news/owns/hz2_en.htm.*

Websites
Asia Week
http://www.asiaweek.com
News magazine

Asif Zardari Website
http://www.asif-zardari.com
Follows his legal problems

CNN Interactive
http://edition.cnn.com
"Newsmaker Profiles," news articles

Dawn: the Internet Edition
http://www.dawn.com
Pakistani newspaper

Gifts of Speech. Sweet Briar College
http://gos.sbc.edu
Speech archive; several by Bhutto

Human Rights Watch
http://www.hrw.org/reports/1999/pakistan/Pakhtml
Report on Pakistan

INQ7
http://www.inq7.net
News service from the Philippines

Jeff Rense Program
http://www.rense.com
News service

MSNBC
http://www.msnbc.com/news
News service

The New York Times Archives
http://www.nytimes.com
News articles

The Oxford Union
http://www.oxford-union.org

Pakistan People's Party
http://www.ppp.org.pk and
http://www.pppuk.com
Official party site; speeches, news, editorials, biographies

Pakistan Review
http://pakistanreview.com
News magazine; op-ed pieces

PakWatan.com
http://www.pakwatan.com
Tourism site, useful for basic geographic and cultural information

Further Reading

Smart Talk: Women's Lecture Series.
http://www.cincinnati.com/smarttalk/bhutto.html

South Asia Tribune
http://www.satribune.com
Newspaper

Story of Pakistan
http://storyofpakistan.com
Timelines, brief histories and biographies

Telegraph
http://www.telegraph.co.uk/news
British newspaper

Victory News Magazine
http://www.victorynewsmagazine.com
Islamic history and culture; Muslim women

Index

Index

Index

Credits

About the Author

Mercedes Padrino majored in History and Literature at Radcliffe College and earned her teaching degree from Brown University. She worked as a high school and college teacher before turning to writing and translating. She lives with her husband and children outside Philadelphia, where she enjoys gardening, bird watching, and studying local history.